Portraits of White

Endorsements

"Step into a world of exploration and nostalgia with *Portraits of White*. This enchanting book unwraps the timeless magic of Christmas music, with Frances sharing stories that bridge divides, rekindle cherished memories, and infuse our hearts with hope. Hearing her own journey of bringing these songs to life, you'll rekindle your desire to nurture positive faith, embrace the unknown, and bask in the eternal spirit of the holiday season. *Portraits of White* celebrates the universal language of music that captures the essence of Christmas and brings us all closer together."

–Dan Miller, *New York Times* Best Selling Author,
48 Days to the Work You Love, and host of
the 48 Days Podcast

"After working with Frances Drost for a little while, I came to understand that first, she had been sheltered as a child from a large amount of famous music, film, and other well-known things. But what blew me away more than anything was her story and, even more shocking, an aversion to Christmas. Who hates Christmas?

Well, I would say we solved that one! When she showed me a new song that she was working on, I thought it was great, but why not do a whole Christmas album? Break your chains! Explore your greatest fears!

What followed was not just 'another' Christmas album, but a celebration of winter, the Christmas season, the piano itself, and what would become a grand annual stage show that continues to surprise everyone - including Frances!

Portraits of White is more than just an album we made with amazing arrangements, songs, players, orchestra, vocals, top engineers, as well as photography and graphic artistry. It has become a brand and event all unto itself, while also being one of the most interesting and dramatic Christmas stories ever told!"

–**Eric Copeland**, Composer/Executive Producer, Positive Spin Songs and Producer of Portraits of White Album

"The creation of a song is a mystical thing, sometimes prompted by some external source, but often by just a thought quietly whispered to our spirit. It's these external and internal experiences that make the whole creation process mysterious and fascinating. If you've ever wanted to get into the mind of a songwriter, this is the place to start. The sincerity and transparency with which Frances shares her journey through the creation of the songs for *Portraits of White* allows the reader to experience the process with her. But it's not just the process that makes this book so revealing. It is her life experiences, fueling that process, that make *Portraits of White* so emotionally compelling. You will be changed by taking the journey with her."

–**Ed Kee**, Conductor of Portraits of White Concerts (2014-2018)

"Frances Drost discovered early in her songwriting journey that a feeling of lingering melancholy is part of the bargain we all make when we choose to chase this elusive craft of setting words to music. Even for the believing Christian, and even at Christmas (supposedly the happiest time of the year), an honest songwriter knows that we're not all okay during the holidays. And so, through this frank and open musical memoir, Frances shares how music provided her a voice, and guided her past her fears and self-doubt, into the biggest musical adventure of her life, an adventure she calls, "Portraits of White."

–Robert Sterling, Songwriter, Author, Record Producer

"If you've ever struggled with the loss of wonder at Christmas, looking to find deeper purpose, *Portraits of White* will awaken your heart. Frances's storytelling ability draws you in, making it feel like you're sitting with her across the table in her studio. Her words are full of life and restore hope. Through the years I've been moved by the truthful messages in her original Christmas songs. Now we get to hear both the struggles and the inspiration that brought those songs to life. Thank you, Frances, for helping us revive the awe of Christmas."

–Tim Spirk, Pastor

"In 1999, Frances Drost decided to start "skipping Christmas." In her newest offering, *Portraits of White*, Frances invites us to travel along her poignant and personal journey through both the beauty and the pain that the season brings. It is a journey of uneasiness, mystery, and sorrow – but one that ultimately leads her to rejoice in and trust a loving, all sufficient God. You'll be blessed by Frances's raw honesty, transparency, humor, and her resolve to surrender to a sacred space where music and meaningful connections intertwine. Seek and find your one small box!"

–Ellie Lofaro, Bible Teacher, Author, Speaker, Humorist, Founder of Heart Mind & Soul Ministries

"Story is what connects us as human beings, and Frances Drost draws you into speculating about your own life stories. How does one dream up a song, a piece of art, a cure for disease? What is the story behind an event, a moment of joy or grief? Frances has a gift for story that marinates spiritual, philosophical, and experiential ingredients and creates a musical concoction of miracles. You will enjoy reading how her music was birthed and how each birth created new life within her."

–Joanne F. Miller, Author of *Creating a Haven of Peace*, Artist, Speaker

"In a world of Christmas movies and songs where Jesus is so painfully absent, Frances Drost's *Portraits of White* will bring healing to your heart. I loved journeying along with this gifted songwriter and having that night of miracles made new again, the way new fallen snow makes a weary earth a wonderland again."

–**Dee Brestin**, Author of *The Friendships of Women* and
He Calls You Beautiful

"I first met Frances in person at Dan Miller's "Will It Fly" event in Sarasota, Florida. Her ability to capture an audience with her gift of music is extraordinary. I'm confident her writings will do the same. Enjoy this written journey as she unveils the divine guidance that helped shape her path of music and intimate moments at the piano."

–**Dr. Jevonnah Ellison**, Goldman Sachs Scholar,
Dean of Coaching, 48 Days

"Frances is a gifted musician, effective communicator, and engaging entertainer. Her life is built on a firm foundation of faith that has been tested and refined through everyday life experiences. Through both song and prose Frances has the unique ability to draw her audience into a parallel journey of spiritual reflection and introspection. In *Portraits of White* Frances once again candidly opens her heart and in her own distinct style takes you on a roller coaster ride of emotions and events while also keeping your feet on solid ground."

–**Don Shenk**, Executive Director, Gospel Tide
Broadcasting Association

"As members of Frances' "Portraits of White" musical ensemble for nearly ten years now, we can tell you that she's not just one of the most musical people we know, she is truly genuine and sincere. Her very real search for joy in Christmas is a search many burdened with loss have attempted. She managed to dig through the commercial noise that drowns out the quiet heart of Christmas, and to touch our hearts with beautiful new songs that point us to the joy and beauty of the real Christmas story."

–Doug and Amy Cook

Portraits of White is a beautiful and moving exploration of the meaning of Christmas. Frances Drost takes us on a journey through her own life and songwriting, weaving together personal stories, reflections on faith, and original music. The result is a book that is both heartwarming and thought-provoking, a reminder of the true meaning of Christmas.

Here are some specific things I liked about *Portraits of White*:

- Drost's writing is honest and heartfelt. She shares her own struggles and triumphs, and her love of Christmas shines through on every page.
- The book is full of beautiful imagery. Drost paints a vivid picture of the winter landscape, and her descriptions of the Christmas season are both nostalgic and inspiring.
- The original music is a wonderful addition to the book. The songs are both catchy and meaningful, and they help to bring Drost's story to life.

Overall, I highly recommend *Portraits of White* to anyone who loves Christmas, music, or personal stories. It is a book that will stay with you long after you finish reading it."

–Elizabeth Rose Logsdon, Interested Reader

"There is a difference in the musical world between knowing the theory behind music and knowing the artistry of music through expression, passion and soul. In this wonderful story, *Portraits of White*, Frances allows us to see the soul of the artist in ways only an artist truly can."

–Teresa McCloy Coach, Speaker and Author of *Do What Matters - Live Life from Rest not Rush*

Portraits *of* White

HOPE *and* **INSPIRATION**
*for Those Who Struggle
with the Holidays*

Frances Drost

NASHVILLE

NEW YORK • LONDON • MELBOURNE • VANCOUVER

Portraits of White

Hope and Inspiration for Those Who Struggle with the Holidays

Published in New York, New York, by Morgan James Publishing. Morgan James is a trademark of Morgan James, LLC. www.MorganJamesPublishing.com

Proudly distributed by Publishers Group West®.

Morgan James BOGO™

A **FREE** ebook edition is available for you or a friend with the purchase of this print book.

CLEARLY SIGN YOUR NAME ABOVE

Instructions to claim your free ebook edition:
1. Visit MorganJamesBOGO.com
2. Sign your name CLEARLY in the space above
3. Complete the form and submit a photo of this entire page
4. You or your friend can download the ebook to your preferred device

ISBN 9781636983141 paperback
ISBN 9781636983158 ebook
Library of Congress Control Number: 2023947049

Cover and Interior Design by:
Chris Treccani
www.3dogcreative.net

Album Cover Design by:
Erick Anderson Photography

Morgan James PUBLISHING
Builds
with...
Habitat for Humanity®
Peninsula and Greater Williamsburg

Morgan James is a proud partner of Habitat for Humanity Peninsula and Greater Williamsburg. Partners in building since 2006.

Get involved today! Visit: www.morgan-james-publishing.com/giving-back

All music and lyrics for Portraits of White written by Frances Drost © 2013 Frances Drost, BMI, Portraits of White Music, except for Joy to the World—Isaac Watts and Christmas in Black and White Medley—Silent Night—Joseph Mohr, Stopford Augustus Brooke, Angels We Have Heard on High— Edward Shippen Barnes, James Chadwick, God Rest Ye Merry Gentlemen—Author and composer unknown, What Child Is This?—Pietro A. Yon, William Chatterton Dix.

Table of Contents

Acknowledgments xvii

Introduction xxiii

1. Miracles. 1

2. One Small Box 15

3. Song of Joy 31

4. Joy to the World 45

5. What If? 55

6. Portraits of White 63

7. Christmas in Black and White 71

8. MOPS. 79

9. Back to the Heart of Christmas 93

10. Ride in the Sleigh 103

11. You with Me 119

12. Take Another Look 133

Coda: The Enigmatic Prelude 143

Thank You. 147

About the Author 149

Portraits of White Album Credits 153

Endnotes. 155

Acknowledgments

Writing a book is like baring my innermost self, as if turning my body inside out and walking in public. Without the support of those who have stood by me, I might have never dared to step outside. My heartfelt thanks to those who bolstered my courage to see this project through.

To Tom, my husband, for always telling me to 'go for it', no matter what 'it' is. Your support has been indispensable, especially as I enter the book publishing world. Thank you for standing by me through the challenges and pushing through the stress together.

To Eric Copeland, they often say that the true value of goal setting lies not solely in achieving the goals themselves, but who a person becomes along the way. You've not only guided me towards my musical aspirations, you have also left a lasting impression on my personal growth.

To Wayne and Suzy Fox, your strong belief in my Christmas songs sparked the inspiration for me to pen my narrative. It was just the spark I needed.

To Donna Houser, my piano teacher. Before a musician can 'solve riddles' with inspiration from their instrument, they first need to learn to play it skillfully. You provided me with the tools I needed long before I knew how I would use them.

To Dan Miller, it's your farm-kid stories that initially grabbed my attention. Your life's journey continues to inspire me to explore creative avenues beyond my music. The support of you and the 48 Days Eagles Community have played a pivotal role in bringing this book to fruition.

To my remarkable publishing team at Morgan James Publishing, you've transformed what seemed like a daunting process into an achievable and even enjoyable endeavor. David Hancock, your visionary leadership in establishing Morgan James, combined with your humble spirit is deeply appreciated. Isaiah Taylor, your suggestion to submit my story is the reason this book is becoming a reality. Jim Howard, Tom Dean, and Addy Normann, your guidance during our first mastermind meeting, infused with a clear vision for presenting this book to the marketplace, immediately assured me that I was in capable hands.

To the dedicated graphic team at Morgan James Publishing, Chris Treccani and Bethany Marshall–whose artistry and design have breathed life into the narrative through colors and visual elements.

To my editor, Stacey Covell at One Word Editing, for skillfully helping me organize my thoughts. A heartfelt thanks also goes to Andrea Stunz at One Word Editing, whose meticulous proofreading and fresh perspective added a valuable layer of polish.

A special thanks to Tracy Mertes and Kendra Angle, whose contributions of their own writing have enriched this story.

Lastly, to my dear brother, Nathan. I've filled these pages with the journey I've been on since you departed. Your absence is keenly felt.

To my siblings:

Doug, Adriel, Aspen, and Nathan.

Let's do Christmas.

Introduction

In the stillness of my music-filled sanctuary, I find myself drawn to the ancient words of Psalm 49:4. The verse speaks of listening carefully to many proverbs and solving riddles with inspiration from a harp. The words offer me an intriguing hint. My heart harbors many complex unsolved riddles. The notion of music serving as a remedy for these intricate dilemmas fascinates me. Awaiting resolution, I am ripe for the embrace of inspiration.

As a songwriter and musician, I am increasingly intrigued by the power of music to uncover wisdom and solve mysteries. When I sit at the piano, it's as if I play the role of a musical detective, piecing together clues and finding answers to the questions that linger inside me. The authors of Psalm 49, the sons of Korah, seem to have observed this truth long before I started to recognize it in myself. They were on to something.

In the secret realms of my spirit (and music studio), I am gradually beginning to understand the powerful key music holds for unlocking the mysteries that plague me. With each note played, I am not just learning how to improve my technique: I am learning how to solve riddles, emotional riddles. In my quiet times, the piano becomes my faithful companion, guiding me through the complicated maze of my emotions. I am training my heart to pay attention to the musical patterns I play, guided by the Holy Spirit's nudges.

Holidays hold a certain sadness for me, but I can't quite grasp why. It's one riddle that often consumes my thoughts. At the age of 33, I made a daring decision to confront this enigma head-on, even though I had no idea where the journey would lead.

With resolute determination, I set out on a mission to decipher the cryptic truths behind the melancholy that overshadowed the holiday season. Along the way, I noted the twists and turns, the moments of revelation, and the whispers of divine guidance that would ultimately lead me to the answers I was seeking. The notes revealed themselves in the form of songs. Unbeknownst to me at the time, the songs would become an album—*Portraits of White*—an audio journal of my courage to confront the riddles of Christmas.

This book unveils the twists, revelations, and divine guidance that shaped my path toward understanding. It is a collection of stories, reflections, and song lyrics that emerged from my intimate moments at the piano, inviting you to witness the culmination of years of struggle, reflection, joy, pain, and revelation.

A fan of the *Portraits of White* album once told me, "Frances, these songs were divinely inspired."

I'll let you decide.

1.

Miracles

Don't judge your feelings, notice them.
Use them as your map.
—Lori Gottlieb

"Psst ... over here."

It was early September 1999. Whispers permeated the air, beckoning me closer, their secretive tones captivating my attention. Amidst the bustling Christmas shop, a radiant aura enveloped a humble display of wooden figurines, surpassing the allure of glimmering decorations. Compelled by their striking simplicity, I was drawn towards them, feeling an otherworldly presence emanating from these miniature carvings. Outside the store, in the picturesque town of Ephrata, Pennsylvania, the September sun bid farewell to a day adorned with perfect weather.

1

The intricately carved beings in the shop had assumed a larger-than-life persona, like the characters from a *Night at the Museum* adventure. Their existence teemed with a sacred message, as if they possessed significant insight meant just for me.

"Contemplate your experiences of Christmas. There are alternative paths to explore," their ethereal voices echoed softly.

Did these wooden entities comprehend my disillusionment with Christmas? It felt premature to ponder December, when September was just getting started. Yet, surrounded by towering artificial trees, ostentatiously adorned and illuminating the Christmas room, the holiday fervor had commenced. Like a kitten entranced by the glittery baubles dangling from the trees, I was normally easily captivated. But on this day, I turned away from the flashy temptations, unimpressed. I yearned for deeper meaning.

The wooden nativity scene on the store shelf now had my full attention, offering the contrast I was seeking. I paused to contemplate a fresh approach to all things related to Christmas.

Each year, I braced myself for the holiday marathon, fraught with questions. What gift will I buy for my husband, Tom? (After only a decade of marriage, I was already running out of creative ideas.) How could I evade the obligatory cookie-baking endeavors? Would it be so terrible to buy cookies for once?

"Yes," my mother's voice, advocating for homemade everything, reverberated within my mind.

Then there was my own holiday wish list—a longing for more twinkling lights, a romantic place to showcase them, greater interior space to accommodate an array of luminosity, and an abundance of funds to acquire additional twinkling lights.

As the music director of a church, on a spiritual level, I wondered where I would summon the energy to orchestrate meaningful services with fresh renditions of familiar carols year after year. I juggled special music, choirs, children, and props for our programs. The Advent candles also perplexed me—always forgetting the order of themes, questioning whether the pink candle symbolized hope or love. I was ashamed of my annual reliance on Google to decipher the Advent themes. Knowing my propensity for clumsiness, I would delegate the lighting of the candles to volunteers, hoping to avoid setting the Advent wreath on fire. No matter how hard I tried to rein myself in, each year, I inevitably succumbed to the avalanche of holiday pressures. Still, I strived to embody the archetypal "Christmas Christian"—the epitome of joy, hospitality, generosity, creativity, spirituality, and awe.

The on-ramp to Christmas promised to lead directly to joy, resembling the anticipation of an impending blizzard of the century (which never failed to elicit pure delight within me). When it came to snowstorms, I reveled in the flurry of preparations, rearranging my schedule and stocking up on essentials—eggs, milk, butter, and chocolate—

from the local grocery store. In the checkout line, I'd over-hear neighbors grumbling about the impending storm. In public and at home, I suppressed my excitement, not wanting to spoil the dread of others regarding the snowy doom, as they seemed to view it. Those of us who adore snow are members of a secret club, covertly celebrating our shared affinity.

Tom, my snow grinch, originally from Michigan, did not share my love for snow and was not part of the secret snow club. It meant more work for him. Grumbling and growling, he'd tuck away his beloved welding shop toys—the Bobcat, tele handler, and various machinery awaiting repair. While I eagerly anticipated the winter extravaganza of white, he was the reluctant snow guardian, valiantly protecting his machinery from the icy clutches of Jack Frost. I understood. I kept my love for snow to myself.

Beyond the groceries and welding shop, we also needed to ensure that our basement woodpile was ample to fuel the hungry wood-burning stove during the storm. Then we'd retire to bed, where I anticipated waking up to a winter wonderland.

Instead, I woke up to a mere dusting of snow. Tom was happy.

Much like the snowy letdown, my idealized Christmas remained a dream yet to be realized. In my heart, I held a vision of the perfect Christmas, with my parents and my siblings all together—a cherished dream I cannot recall ever experiencing. It may have happened, but I can't remember (probably due to the fact that I'm the youngest in the family). As a child, for many years, I longed for the unity of family—physical and emotional togetherness. And oh yes, lots of presents under the tree. Or better yet, a mountain of presents!

As I stood in the Ephrata Christmas shop, I began to recognize the semblance between the promise of Christmas and the sparkling ornaments. The allure of the ornaments began to fade, and in its place, I felt the desire for something deeper. In that moment of contemplation, newly aware of my dormant desires, I was struck by the notion that the only way to truly find Christmas was to purposefully skip it. And so, in that moment, I made a resolute decision. I would officially forgo Christmas.

To me, skipping Christmas entailed liberating myself from the stress-inducing traditions—things like gifts, cookies, and decorations. I sought emotional detachment from the commercial aspects of the holiday, craving space to redefine my relationship with Christmases past and explore the spiritual treasures of the current season.

As a music director in a church, I couldn't completely detach from church activities and programs. However, I resolved to shed everything else. Fortunately, my husband wholeheartedly embraced the plan, likely thrilled to be spared the daunting task of gift selection.

It was astonishing to realize that a wooden nativity scene in a Christmas shop served as the catalyst for this departure from tradition. The enchantment of the nativity story had waned, likely due to numerous years of amateur reenactments during church programs—programs that I eagerly participated in when I was a little girl. Homemade angel costumes crafted from white bed sheets, embellished with golden tinsel halos, and ill-fitting flannel bathrobes borrowed from the parents of cast members had ceased to charm me. I now preferred elegant dresses, not billowing white sheets and gaudy garlands. If given the choice, I would have opted for a more refined setting than a stable to give birth to a child. Perhaps the Hilton, if available!

As I processed this new endeavor, I decided my mission would be to reintroduce myself to the biblical narrative. I would immerse myself in the story as much as possible before December 25th arrived. Through countless readings of Luke's gospel, the childhood bathrobe version of the nativity tale gradually started to fade away. In its place, a gentle sense of wonder began to take hold. I wanted to nurture a unique bond with a timeless narrative full of miracles. I craved my own miracle.

A miracle is "an event that appears inexplicable by the laws of nature and so is held to be supernatural in origin or an act of God: *'Miracles are spontaneous, they cannot be summoned, but come of themselves'* (Katherine Anne Porter)."[1] As I dove deeper into the nativity story, I discovered a season teeming with concentrated supernatural occurrences. Miracles heralded the birth of Jesus and followed in its wake—a succession of extraordinary events, like special baby showers before the ultimate shower.

Dreams (and in some cases, angels) revealed specific details: the gender and names of babies (John and Jesus), the resolution of Cousin Elizabeth's barrenness, the anticipation of social shame because of Mary's pregnancy, prophecies about kingship, heartbreak, guidance, admonishment, timing, and Zechariah's supernatural muteness.

While the story continued to unfold, a subtle but astounding detail caught my attention. In a remarkable encounter, two unborn cousins, nestled in their respective mother's wombs, seemed to share a recognition that surpassed the boundaries of time and flesh. It was in the intimate space of Elizabeth's belly that John, sensing the presence of his cousin Jesus, responded with a remarkable physical reaction. As someone who has experienced the heartache of losing two siblings, this shed light on something I had already been pondering: do our spirits possess an innate ability to forge connections not only after our loved ones have departed, but even before they take their first breath in this world?

The big supernatural crescendo of the story came in the form of a heavenly display, when even the stars had to move aside as a myriad of angels took center stage. It made such a commotion that the shepherds (and probably the sheep) shook! A string of miracles, all leading to one exceptional event—Jesus's birth.

As I documented these wondrous occurrences, counting them one by one in the New Living Translation, I tallied a total of thirty-seven miracles. It was inspiring. In this fertile ground of ancient stories, my creative songwriting heart stirred.

Then one day, as I was running errands, I tuned in to *Adventures in Odyssey*, a popular radio program known for its engaging storytelling. On that particular day, the program was highlighting the nativity story. As I listened to the dramatized version, the characters Connie and Eugene found themselves mysteriously transported back in time to the very heart of the manger scene. Instantly, the nativity story sprang to life in a vivid and uniquely personal way for me.

Seated in the confines of my vehicle, I was transfixed by the radio waves carrying the immersive drama. It was as if I could feel the same awe and wonder that Connie and Eugene experienced. The words I had been reading in the Bible now spoke to me, inviting me to share in the sights, sounds, and emotions of that sacred night in Bethlehem. The miracles I had studied became vivid and tangible, unfolding before me in real time. With each passing moment, the story's progression evoked emotions that welled up inside Eugene (and me). Connie aptly summed it all up in one short phrase: "This has been a night of miracles."[2]

Those words echoed in my mind as I turned off the radio. I sat there, letting them wash over me in a moment of silence. Then, so gently, I felt a sweet sense of inspiration stirring. I had started writing a song a few weeks earlier based on my close examination of the ancient story. The song, which was almost finished, just needed one last touch. In this case, that touch was as simple as finding the right title for the song. Connie's words were just what I needed. I decided to call my song "A Night of Miracles."

♪

In the recording studio, we usually give songs a working title for quick reference. So what started as "A Night of Miracles" became "Miracles." Feeling like the shorter title was a better fit for the song, I kept it as the final title.

The year 1999 will always hold a special place in my heart. It was a year untouched by the conventional trappings, allowing the free flow of song ideas. It was during this time that I first began to dream of recording a Christmas album. Fast forward to 2013, and that dream started to materialize as I planned to start recording in Nashville.

As the saying goes, "It all begins with a song." As we prepared to work on the album, a stroke of serendipity occurred. "Miracles" would be the first song we'd record. From the instant the band struck their first notes on what is affectionately called "tracking day," I was enamored with the way the musicians interpreted my masterpiece. I could hear every instrument distinctly because each instrument had its own track.

The rhythm section, consisting of drums, guitars, bass guitars, and keyboards, laid down the groove. The band played in perfect synchrony, guided by the steady pulse of a click track. Do you remember those piano lessons where it was a struggle to follow the monotonous ticktock of the metronome? Nashville session musicians possess a remarkable ability to balance astounding accuracy, faithfully adhering to a relentless ticktock with breathtaking creativity.

Imagine a troupe of ballerinas, gracefully twirling in unison, their movements flawlessly synchronized, all while delicately poised on a tightrope—keeping pace with the incessant and, admittedly, obnoxious clicking noise. Like dancers, the musicians were a sight to behold, magnificent in their craft. It's no wonder my producer handpicked the cream of the crop, the renowned "A-team" of Nashville. Their expertise was worth every penny.

Once tracking day was over, my producer sent me a rough mix of the song, seeking my approval of the general feel. I listened to the song and joyfully danced around my living room as the sound of tinkling bells enveloped me. I loved the groove of the song, but I really loved the sounds of the little bells. In my grand vision of what the Christmas spirit should feel like, this was it! The kind that fostered boundless possibilities.

"Don't get too attached to the initial mix," my producer, Eric, had warned. But it was too late. I was already attached to those bells.

Lest you think my producer was a killjoy, you should know that the rough mix from tracking day lacks the polished balance of instrument volumes. Consequently, it was possible that the bells I was hearing would not make the final cut. Even if they did, it was also possible that they could become subtle undertones blended into the symphony of other instruments and vocals added later on. The bells could end up being mostly felt rather than explicitly heard. I eagerly awaited the outcome.

My manager, Wally Nason, shared his perspective on the Christmas songs I had crafted. According to him, "Miracles" held a special place at the top of the list. He had been a part of my music journey long enough to witness its evolution and my growth as a writer. In his opinion, he considered the song one of my finest compositions.

It's important to recognize that songwriting is a personal and subjective craft, and opinions can vary. Nonetheless, receiving praise from Wally (who was known for being painfully—yet constructively blunt in his assessments) greatly boosted my confidence and pushed me closer towards my dream of becoming a skilled and accomplished songwriter.

In the end, the tinkling bells made the final cut.

Merry Christmas to me.

Miracles

by Frances Drost

Long awaited holy one

It was written You would come

We've been waiting so have You

Is it true is it true

Barren woman giving birth

Virgin Mary motherhood

God is speaking in a young man's dreams

Trust in me trust in me

A night of miracles is taking place

God has come in amazing ways

Angels appearing shepherds rejoicing

Oh what a night this will be

Oh what a night this will be

Baby Jesus in Mary's arms

Old man waiting in the temple yard

God had promised he would see this day

Celebrate celebrate

A night of miracles is taking place

God has come in amazing ways

Angels appearing shepherds rejoicing

Oh what a night this will be

Oh what a night this will be

Glory to God in the highest

Peace and good will to all men

A night of miracles is taking place

God has come in amazing ways

Angels appearing shepherds rejoicing

Oh what a night this will be

Oh what a night this will be

2.

One Small Box

*Following our inner compass will usually
benefit the whole community.*
—"Snowflake" Bentley

I sat at the fundraising dinner, immersed in a story about the power of one. The speaker's voice filled the room, talking about a man named Charlie.

Charlie Byers was a man with a vision, a man who believed in the potential of one radio broadcast to change lives. In 1946, just after World War II, he launched a radio program called *The Gospel Tide*. When I was growing up, I would hear my mother rave about Charlie and the influence he had on her spiritual journey. But it wasn't until that fundraising dinner that I truly understood the magnitude of Charlie's vision.

15

The speaker continued, sharing the remarkable expansion of The Gospel Tide Broadcasting Association. Starting as a small-town program, it had spread its reach to Africa and India, using indigenous speakers to broadcast the Gospel message in different languages. However, there was a challenge in India—many people lacked access to radios or couldn't afford them.

The story took an unexpected turn when the speaker told about a young girl in India who had listened to the broadcast in Hindi at her uncle's home. Later, she reached out to the United States office for more information about Christianity. In her heartfelt letter, she mentioned that her family couldn't afford a radio, so they couldn't listen to the program at home.

Moved by her plea, a generous friend of the ministry provided a radio for the young girl. She wrote again, expressing her gratitude and sharing the incredible news that the lives of her entire family had been transformed by the messages they heard from the broadcast because they received a radio.

The speaker's words resonated with me, especially when he mentioned a specific amount: $40. With that donation, people like the young girl in India could be given radios and hear about God's love for them. The tangible impact of this small amount gripped me. An idea began to form in my mind—a song about boxes, small packages, and something big coming from something small, like a radio.

Charlie's vision left an imprint on me. By the early 1990s, I had started writing songs and harbored a secret desire to do something more with them. Thanks to Charlie's radio program, I didn't have to wait very long.

It was in September 1994, at Forge Recording Studios in Valley Forge, Pennsylvania, that I had my first taste of recording. I didn't realize the career-altering impact that single day would have on me until a conversation with my husband a few weeks later. Still floating in a state of euphoria and adrenaline, I struggled to come back to reality.

"Are you ever going to come down from there?" My husband's voice snapped me out of my reverie.

"I need you ... here," he reminded me of the present moment and the need for my attention to matters at home.

If anyone was to blame for my newfound obsession with recording (beyond Charlie), it was Lenny Gault. Lenny was a Nashville-country-singer-turned-pastor who introduced me to the world of recording. Although he lived just a few hours from me in Pennsylvania, he made frequent trips to Nashville as a country music recording artist. Lenny had been approached by the director of Charlie's broadcast to record inspirational songs for their program and needed a piano player.

In what must have been the hand of providence, I got a phone call. Lenny remembered me as the "red-headed piano player" from a small country church who had accompanied him for a concert when his regular pianist had suddenly become ill. Lenny shared that there had been a musical synergy between us in that one short meeting and concert experience. I couldn't deny that I had felt it, too. He asked if I could accompany him for the recording project. The man could sing. I could play the piano. It was an easy yes.

The circumstances had aligned in a truly remarkable way. The financial constraints of the recording project necessitated a search for a recording studio closer to home in Pennsylvania, bypassing Lenny's usual pilgrimage to Nashville. This unique turn of events opened a door of opportunity for me, allowing me to step foot into the magnetic (and even a tad hypnotic) world of recording for the very first time.

But oh the challenges I faced! Perhaps my easy yes was a tad naïve. I quickly discovered that a one-off concert was not the same as preparing for a recording. Getting ready for recording felt like stepping onto a huge stage, where every note and rhythm had to come together perfectly. It required careful commitment and intense concentration. Practice was only the beginning.

Our rehearsals became trials for me. Lenny, an older, peculiar, and rotund man, struggled to breathe due to health issues and required frequent breaks. His storytelling habits ate up valuable practice time, leaving me feeling frustrated and unproductive. Sensing my growing displeasure, Lenny tried to enlighten me about Nashville's ways, emphasizing the importance of chit-chat and breathers between songs. However, his "breathers" seemed excessively long. And besides that, Nashville held little meaning to me at this point. It was just a distant universe somewhere in the South—was it in Tennessee? Who cared?!

Another obstacle was the absence of written music or chord charts. I improvised arrangements on the fly and played songs in any key, as demanded by Lenny. The mastermind behind the madness, he would throw me musical loop-de-loops and request songs in bizarre keys, leaving me feeling like a pianist riding through an avant-garde key signature maze. My musical training and talent had its limits, and navigating the rollercoaster pushed me to the brink of hysteria. On any given day, he'd want the song just a half step up, the next day, a half step down, leaving me stranded in keys as unfamiliar to me as a kazoo concerto. It was a wild ride, to say the least!

During one particular story session, Lenny warned about musicians crumbling under studio pressure. *No kidding! Would I withstand the test?* The stakes were high, as we had to record ten songs in a single day for the radio program. The pressure was intense. To top it off, at the last minute, Lenny also suggested I sing harmony with him in the studio, which meant coming up with more musical ideas beyond the piano.

What? Not only did I have to navigate the piano in unknown keys, but now I was also expected to sing. It was like conducting a grand orchestra with my fingertips and belting out tunes with my vocal cords while playing the tuba. The piano itself held enough weight and responsibility, and I certainly didn't need another element adding to the intricacy of our musical masterpiece.

The twenty-four hours leading up to recording day intensified as I started to feel physically unwell. Is it any wonder? (In hindsight, it was undoubtedly a severe bout of nerves). Filled with a sense of urgency to ease my discomfort, my mother drove over to my house the night before we were to record and gave me one of her ancient laxative pills. Not wanting to be wasteful, she still had a bottle left over from the bygone era of the 1960s. Oh the curious treasures of her vintage medicine cabinet!

Whether it was the pill or some studio magic in the air, the moment I put on the headphones and played the first song alongside Lenny's deep and resonant Merle Haggard-like voice, the next morning, the pressure dissolved. I entered the euphoric state of the merry land of Oz.

Inside the studio, I soared. The professional headphones enveloped me in surround sound, blocking out the world and leaving only music in my ears. Lenny's lush voice reached new heights through the professional microphone. The melodies, grand piano resonance, and my improvised arrangements put me in a trance-like state. I wanted more of "that."

I played the piano for hours, relying on my hastily scribbled notes, keeping up with Lenny, and adding background harmonies. The studio's synthesizer offered orchestral sounds, which I utilized to sprinkle violin, flute, and string pads into the mix. We did ten songs, plus vocals and additional touches. When the day was over, surprisingly, I had not only withstood the pressure, but craved more of it. The adrenaline surge made me forget about food, a sign that I had transcended normal functioning.

Emerging from the studio was a bittersweet moment. When we paused for dinner on our journey back home, my stomach reveled in satisfying fare, while my heart remained tethered to the studio's creative energy. My mind felt like a whirlwind of chaos, leaving me grappling to string coherent thoughts together and articulate them with clarity. I was beyond exhausted.

On the journey home, I withdrew into my own thoughts, contemplating what I could do to keep this feeling. I even thought about cleaning toilets in the studio if it meant being able to hang out there on a permanent basis.

Back at home, as the days passed, my husband witnessed a side of me he had never seen before. He hadn't been able to go with me to the studio and I couldn't find the words to explain what I was experiencing. It created an unfamiliar dynamic. I had no one to help me bridge the gap. (I have since observed this phenomenon with other recording artists. Recording changes you somehow.) This otherworldly experience marked the beginning of a cycle—highs and lows, and the rush of adrenaline followed by the crash. I would eventually accept that it was a normal part of the recording artist's journey.

Lenny's vivid tales of his past recording adventures in Nashville began to resonate. As the dust settled after my inaugural recording experience, I finally understood what he meant when he told me he would retreat to the darkness of his basement after his musical adventures. The prospect of resuming a normal life felt like a daunting task. Going back home was difficult.

Over the next few months, my adrenaline rush eventually subsided, but a residual feeling of wanting to make my mark and share my music with the world remained. I couldn't shake it. I poured myself into writing songs. While my husband may not have fully understood the ebb and flow of my emotional journey, he offered steadfast support and encouraged me to keep following my heart.

Two years later, feeling ready to record a project of my own, I returned to Forge Recording Studios. I quickly learned that gaining access to the studio didn't require scrubbing toilets. It simply involved writing a check—a familiar concept known as "paying to play" in the music industry.

With my new project underway, I focused on one of my songs called "The Willow." Inspired by Psalm 137, this ancient tale recounts the plight of the captive Jewish people who found themselves in a foreign land. Sitting beside the rivers of Babylon, they grappled with the temptation to abandon their musical instruments, hang their harps on the willow trees, and surrender to sorrow. It had special significance for me, as it spoke about resilience and the refusal to give up when faced with adversity. In my state of songwriting bliss, I was unprepared for the magnitude of the trial looming on the horizon.

I savored the rough mix cassette tape of "The Willow" from the studio, playing it often in my new van. The van was a wonderful gift from friends in Michigan who had originally planned to sell it and give my husband and me the money. However, when they couldn't find a buyer, they decided to bless us with the van instead. It was an answer to my prayers, as I had been seeking a vehicle to transport my sound equipment to events. My music ministry was growing.

On a September night, feeling full of joy and gratitude, I drove my new van home from a memorable fundraising dinner for The Tide program. Accompanying me on this tranquil, reflective ride through the lush Pennsylvania countryside were two revered figures. Charlie, the esteemed founder, sat across from me in the front, and Maurice Bender, the director, was behind me in the back seat.

As we cruised along the dark country roads, I cherished the fact that I now had a means of transporting my equipment and accommodating others. It was an incredible feeling, like a newfound independence liberating me from relying on others for transportation. My grand keyboard was in the back of the van, while the cassette tape of my new song lived in the tape deck. Everything seemed perfect. I was reveling in the evening's bliss and the blessing of sharing it with Charlie and Maurice. I had found my sweet spot, a sacred space where music and meaningful connections intertwine.

Suddenly, as we were crossing a bridge over the Pennsylvania Turnpike, a car appeared at the top of the hill, swerving recklessly from one side of the road to the other. My mind raced as I tried to anticipate its trajectory, clutching onto a flicker of hope that it would miraculously bypass us unscathed. However, with two cars firmly positioned in front of us, we were trapped with nowhere to escape on the bridge.

With a deafening crash, our van came to an abrupt halt, glass shattering around us. The immediate aftermath was met with eerie silence—a moment frozen in time. Maurice later recounted the vivid memory of the headlights bearing down on us from the front left corner of the car, followed by the collision that left us all wondering if we were alright. The two cars preceding us were nowhere to be seen.

Cars behind us stopped, and concerned strangers approached our van. My first thought was for Charlie, whose failing vision had prevented him from seeing the oncoming car. I had to check on him. As I stepped out of the van, I felt a searing pain in my shoulder, my hand instinctively clutching it. A concerned stranger noticed my discomfort and asked if I was okay. I muttered a feeble reassurance, trying to mask my pain.

Emergency vehicles soon arrived, their lights flashing in the darkness. Amidst the chaos, an officer approached us and uttered words that still resonate in my mind, "You should all be dead. Your seatbelts must be the only thing that saved you." It was a chilling reminder of the fine line between life and death.

Maurice appeared to have a few bumps and scrapes, but Charlie was seriously injured. A helicopter soon arrived to whisk him away to the hospital, while I was taken to a local ER for examination. My memory of the night is fragmented, with only snippets remaining. I had to return to

the hospital later for a head examination because of concerns of a possible brain bleed based on X-rays.

In the days that followed, fear gripped me whenever I
contemplated getting into a vehicle. The traumatic experience had left me haunted by the mere sight of oncoming
traffic, regardless of their position on the road. Our beloved
van, the gift that symbolized my newfound freedom, was
now reduced to wreckage. I could no longer bring myself
to play "The Willow."

Charlie's valiant battle and time in the hospital per-
sisted until December 17, 1996, when he passed away at
age eighty-eight. He left behind an enormous void in the
hearts of all who knew him. It was Charlie, the very catalyst of the broadcast, who extended his voice and hands to
touch lives as far as the distant shores of India, even inspiring the likes of the "red-headed girl from Green Spring" in
Newville, PA. How could it be that his ministry came to
an end just as mine was beginning to flourish and bloom?

When his family graciously invited me to provide
piano music during his memorial service, it was both an
honor and an emotional undertaking. In the face of such
great loss, I was deeply humbled by the remarkable grace
and kindness extended to me by Charlie's family, a testa-
ment to the enduring legacy of this truly significant man.

Nine years later, in 2005, I received an invitation to
return and perform at the fundraising dinners for The
Tide. It was during one of these events that the new director shared the story about the young girl in India who

didn't have access to a radio, which inspired me to write the song "One Small Box."

Throughout my songwriting journey, I had been no stranger to the impact of personal experiences on my lyrics. My producer had pointed out my inclination to weave themes of death into my songs, often prompting me to rewrite my lyrics in a more hopeful tone. This brought to mind a verse I had originally penned for "One Small Box," which resonates with the spirit of my storytelling.

In the early drafts, the words painted a picture of a rainy day and a tear-stained face, depicting a widow standing by her husband's grave. It was a stark portrayal of a lifetime of promises extinguished, as her beloved was laid to rest in an old pine box. In hindsight, as I now collate these song stories and my life experiences, I cannot escape the haunting question of whether the far-reaching impact of the accident, which left me burdened with a sense of partial responsibility for the loss of such an extraordinary man, had a far more indelible effect on my soul than I had initially realized.

However, it's essential to remember that life's twists and turns, even its darkest moments, often pave the way for unexpected blessings and immense growth. Despite the challenges I have faced, my passion for music and the undeniably clear sense of calling toward it have kept me going. And with time, that commitment has opened more doors of opportunity. And all of this from one man's vision and one small box.

One Small Box

by Frances Drost

Candlelight and a single rose

Set the tone for his love proposed

Lifetime of promises

Made to the one he loves

All wrapped up in a velvet box

Something big from something small is

Nothing short of a miracle

Look and see the loving thoughts

Wrapped inside that one small box

Daddy's watching his little girl

Ribbons hang in her golden curls

Opening packages

Finally she gets to his

How she loves her music box

Something big from something small is

Nothing short of a miracle

Look and see the loving thoughts

Wrapped inside that one small box

Heaven's King coming here to earth

Not the way you would think He'd work

True love and joy to us

Sweet baby Jesus

Wrapped in clothes in an old feed box

Something big from something small is

Nothing short of a miracle

Look and see the loving thoughts

Wrapped inside that one small box

Village sits by the radio

It's all they have of a way to know

Good news and hopefulness

Promise of life it gives

Coming through that magic box

Something big from something small is

Nothing short of a miracle

Look and see the loving thoughts

Wrapped inside that one small box

3.

Song of Joy

Life can only be understood backwards;
but it must be lived forwards.
—Soren Kierkegaard

Walking through peaceful grounds years after the
battle, the soldiers can still hear the cannons.
—Richard Paul Evans

Keeping a journal has been my lifeline, an intimate refuge where I pour out the depths of my soul. The ritual began when I was twelve years old, likely absorbed through osmosis from my sister and father, who were both dedicated journal keepers.

Growing up, my sister and I shared a bedroom, our own haven of secrets and dreams. Though we respected each other's privacy, I couldn't help but wonder what hidden truths lay within the pages of her journal. We respectfully refrained from delving into each other's written words, a pact sealed by love and trust. As we age, we are somewhat cracking the door to our secret writings when we selectively share little tidbits from our journals with each other. It's such a special gift.

Within the pages of my journals, a complex tapestry of emotions unfolds, creating an intricate emotional seismograph—a tangible map of my life's seismic activity. These cherished records hold more than mere facts; they serve as a compass, guiding me through the fault lines of my emotions. Over the course of decades, patterns have emerged, offering guidance and a flicker of hope as I navigate the intricate complexities of life. Using pen and paper, journaling helps me figure myself out.

My father meticulously chronicled his days in a diary, using a self-designed shorthand system that intrigued me as a young girl. I paid little attention to the details of his record-keeping, but after his passing, a deep curiosity awakened in me. Consumed by grief, I felt a longing to peer into his written legacy.

What wisdom did he possess? How did he navigate the treacherous waters of grief when my brother, Nathan, tragically drowned? And how did he find strength in the face of the heart-wrenching news when my other brother Doug succumbed to a fatal tractor accident? As his daughter, I sought answers, hoping to find comfort and discover hidden truths. Our shared idiosyncrasies bound us together, and I believed his words held the key to unlocking some of my emotional riddles.

My father was more than just a father; he was a kindred spirit, mirroring my quirks and peculiarities. Our connection ran deep, woven into the very fabric of our shared DNA. Within the precious pages of his diaries, I sought to decipher the secret language of our intertwined existence. I believed that by reading them, I could uncover the secrets that would reveal not only who he was but also shed light on my perspective of the world.

One winter night, as the moon, like a radiant conductor, directed beams of light onto everything outside, I sat on our living room floor. Completely engrossed in my father's family letters (which I would later discover were quite different from his diaries), I started making notes. My husband, seated across the room in his recliner bearing the imprints of countless hours, asked, "What on earth are you up to now?"

A mischievous smile crept across my face. "I'm taking notes on Daddy's notes," I said.

Tom, my ever-patient husband, simply rolled his eyes, a gesture that suggested he had long ago accepted my peculiar ways. He already knew I was a tad eccentric, and this latest endeavor only solidified his belief. But I wasn't alone in my idiosyncrasies.

Later, when I shared this amusing anecdote with my sister, we giggled. It turns out she, too, had been indulging in the same habit of meticulously dissecting our father's writings. And wouldn't you know it, her husband also couldn't help but roll his eyes in exasperation (I like to think it's fondness). How nice it was to know that at least one other person out there shared my insatiable curiosity.

When I finally summoned the courage to delve into my father's personal journals, which I hoped would be more personal than his letters, it marked a monumental step in my journey. I was sure they would be filled with introspection and emotional graphs like my own. With an eager but nervous heart, I confronted a blend of anticipation and trepidation.

As I carefully turned the weathered pages of those hardback books, their musty scent intermingling with faint traces of mildew, I was met with a surprising realization—I was unable to decipher the majority of his handwritten entries. Those that were not coded with his secret shorthand were mostly just factual statements. With an unsatisfied curiosity and a heavy heart, I returned the diaries to my basement, their boxes saturated with the lingering scent of untold stories. Years passed.

Then I began writing this book and my curiosity once again stirred. I decided to give my father's secretly coded journals another chance. I would start with the date of my birthday. Surely there would be a few heartfelt sentiments rather than mere facts on that day, I thought. I reached out to my sister and asked if she still had Daddy's shorthand codes. Fortunately, she came to my rescue.

Venturing into the basement and rummaging through boxes of his diaries, I finally laid my hands on his planner from 1966, aptly named *Dailyaid: "The Silent Secretary."*

As I eagerly flipped to the month of April, I discovered a few precious fragments of knowledge about the day of my birth, the 26th of April.

While my mother was at the hospital in labor, he ...

- Ran errands
- Tended to tractor repair (a broken meter cable, etc.)
- Made a bank deposit
- Stopped at the library
- Made phone calls
- Recorded the weather (it was a clear day and 36 degrees Fahrenheit when he made the journal entry).
- After I was born, he mentioned I was cute. *That's worth something!*
- He noted that my mother smiled when they told her I was a girl.

The list continued…

- He got the plow and tractor ready.
- Two rounds of something planted (Oats perhaps?)
- My brother Adriel had his piano lesson that night.

The last entry of the page said that "B. (Bertha is my mother) called and said baby has yellow jaundice and may be transferred …"

Scribbled in the far corner of the bottom of the page, he recorded that he went to bed at 11:00 p.m.

In the whimsical realm of babyhood, I wondered what time I bid the world goodnight on that first night.

In those faded, time-stained pages, I discovered glimpses of my father's life, his daily routines, and the mundane details that composed his existence. While it may not have been the treasure trove of emotions and revelations I yearned for, it provided a sort of fragmented manuscript of our shared history.

Apparently, my father wasn't the only one keeping records. According to Psalm 56:8, God also keeps meticulous records, a fact that has brought me comfort. I wrote about it in my own journal:

October 17, 2000:
Psalm 56:8 "You keep track of all my sorrows. You have collected all my tears in Your bottle. You have recorded each one in Your book."

I have to wonder when I read this what God keeps all these records for. I am encouraged to know that He sees all my sorrows—all my tears. He notices when I cry. Surely His attention to me is not in vain.

Perhaps God keeps records because He understands the power of the pen. In my own life, I viewed ink as my conduit for expression, a path to bring balance to the turbulent waves of my soul. It smoothed the rough edges and unraveled the depths of the sorrow and joyless existence that haunted my past. But even in 1999, when Christmas lost its sparkle, though I was gradually becoming aware of the presence of sorrow, I didn't understand the extent of my joylessness until I was entrusted with a significant task: writing a song about joy.

As the Director of Worship, my role involved sharing the load of service planning with other talented musicians within the church. To foster creativity and spiritual growth among the fellow musicians, I delegated some of the planning responsibilities. Each of us took turns curating services, a seemingly brilliant arrangement.

One of the musicians made an unusual request: she asked me to compose a song about joy, drawing inspiration from Isaiah 35. I found myself taken aback. I had hoped to lighten my workload, not take on additional tasks. Yet, the appeal of songwriting proved irresistible. "Sure," I said confidently, "I will write a song about joy. No problem."

But joy, like a rainbow's end, had been eluding me. Now, charged with writing this song, I became keenly aware of the scope of its scarcity in my life. Deemed a fruit of the Spirit, I struggled to figure out how to actually be joyful. Reading the prophetic words of Isaiah's passage on joy forced me to confront my own joyless existence.

Years later, armed with the meticulous records of my journal and the clarity that comes with age (now climbing toward my mid-fifties), I can look back and see there was something that brought me joy—music. The act of writing, creating, recording, and performing music brought incredible pleasure. However, beyond the realm of melodies and harmonies, joy lived at the end of the rainbow, beside the pot of gold.

Fortunately, a theory started emerging, born from my lifelong observations documented inside the pages of my journal. As a pianist who started playing by ear as a toddler, I believe the ability to "hear" resonated across other aspects of life. In the tapestry of my family's history, one interwoven with an abundance of sadness, I had unknowingly learned to discern the subtle strains of sadness echoing year after year.

> *March 22, 2020:*
> *My ear is so sensitive—not just physically, but emotionally. I can "hear" things around me that others don't hear. I could hear the depth of sadness our family was living through—both spiritually and emotionally. It went deep down into my soul. It had to come out somewhere … came out in my songwriting … and led me to write about my despair concerning Christmas.*

> *March 22, 2020:*
> *If I hadn't been listening, maybe I would be singing a different tune. I started out playing the piano by ear. But my ears heard more than they should and I began playing minor songs/notes.*

November 12, 2018:
Our tendency in life is to want to write the sad
moments out of our lives. I've written songs with sad
moments—perhaps too many of them—but I had to
write them to process life to get to the happy moments.

Going back to being tasked with writing a song about joy for Advent, I had a hurdle to overcome beyond the creative aspect of songwriting. They say one should write what they know, and what I knew all too well was the haunting presence of sadness, sorrow, and grief. It's no wonder that writing from a place of joy was a formidable challenge.

However, with the Advent service clock ticking and the impending task of crafting a song for it, I couldn't afford to wallow in the familiar depths of my emotions. Like a dedicated worker who dutifully clocks in, regardless of their enthusiasm for the job, I approached the piano, pencil in hand, and began to compose.

Drawing inspiration from the scripture passage, I meticulously extracted phrases and conjured a title, "Song of Joy." Once I had a title, the remaining pieces of the song fell into place with greater ease.

In the vein of the prophetic and forward-looking nature of the book of Isaiah, I found myself weaving a tapestry of words that portrayed a time yet to unfold:

"Even the desert will be glad

And the wilderness rejoice

When the Lord comes near"

With the deadline looming, I completed the song just in time for our Advent service. I invited two talented girls from the worship team to join me in singing, savoring the harmonious blend of our voices and the buoyant melody I had created.

Reflecting on that assignment, I can now see that it was a gift—a significant milestone on my journey to find joy. It served as a marker, not quite reaching the destination of pure, exuberant joy, but a clear sign I was on the right path. Since that Christmas, I can now trace back to the time when I composed a song about something I lacked and didn't even comprehend the breadth of my deprivation. I am grateful to have uncovered this revelation.

You might be encouraged to know that in the pages of my journals, there was also evidence of growth. My metaphorical tree, once barren of joy, began to bear fruit. It came gradually. Gently. But it was coming.

December 26, 2011:
Christmas felt a bit different this year—in a good way. The message of the love of the Father is making a difference in me and it's times like this where it really shows up. I sensed the vastness of the gift of

Jesus somehow. The "freeness" of it. It's hard to even put on paper. I just know that I felt more at peace this year. That's an example of a "new thing" springing up and the ability to perceive it! Isaiah 43:19—rivers in desert places.

"Song of Joy" has evolved into a magnificent opening piece for my concerts, skillfully establishing the desired atmosphere and conveying the promise of joy. As I perform it, a remarkable transformation occurs—I genuinely experience joy. Though I didn't consciously "write what you know", I find myself experiencing the joy I penned. Perhaps this mirrors the nature of the prophetic book of Isaiah—foretelling events long before their actual occurrence. I now see that crafting this song was not merely an artistic endeavor, it was a prophetic act for my heart, planting the seeds of joy that would eventually flourish.

Song of Joy
by Frances Drost

Even the desert will be glad and the wilderness rejoice

When the Lord comes near

Then blinded eyes will start to see

And the deaf ears they will hear

When the Lord comes near

Sing a song of hope sing a song of joy

When the glory of the Lord is near

Sing a song of hope sing a song of joy

For the glory of the Lord is here

Then those who know the Lord will sing

On the journey as they go

When the Lord comes near

Gladness and joy will overcome

And the sorrow disappear

When the Lord comes near

Sing a song of hope sing a song of joy

When the glory of the Lord is near

Sing a song of hope sing a song of joy

For the glory of the Lord is here

Do not be afraid I bring you good news great joy to all

To all the people

Today in Bethlehem a savior is born

He is Christ the Lord

He is Christ the Lord

Sing a song of hope sing a song of joy

When the glory of the Lord is near

Sing a song of hope sing a song of joy

For the glory of the Lord is here

4.

Joy to the World

T he first six months of my life were filled with laughter, courtesy of my brother—the family clown. My mother often fondly recounted his natural ability to make me laugh as a baby. Later on, another entertainer entered my life, upholding the tradition of bringing joy: my cousin, Wendell.

There we'd be, engrossed in side-splitting laughter, nestled between a stylish porcelain fixture and a matching sink, on a fashionably plush rug, with just enough space for two youngsters. Without windows, this small space—a bathroom—made a perfect makeshift cinema. We spent many hours tucked away in this most unlikely place.

Distanced from tedious adult conversations, we were free to binge on old Laurel and Hardy movies. As the black and white images flickered on the wall, we got our fill of belly laughs.

My favorite episode involved terraced stairs, a narrow yard, and a cumbersome upright piano. Just as the two bumbling fellows set out to maneuver the large piano up the long flight of outdoor concrete, they were interrupted by a sophisticated woman coming down. She was trying to control the speed of her baby buggy.

Thinking it would only take a minute to stop and help, Laurel and Hardy set the piano down and stepped off the stairs onto the grass. Focused on transporting the stylish lady's buggy, the gentlemen got right to work.

Meanwhile, the piano, as if possessed by its own mischievous spirit, took off, bouncing down the paved stairs. With each bounce, the piano strings strummed, the keys twanged, and the wood creaked as the big music box descended. Landing with a sudden loud clunk, the music jarringly came to an end.

In the bathroom-turned-cinema, our hysterical laughter surely must have slipped out into the rest of the house, but we were too giddy to care. Doubling over, clutching our stomachs, and gasping for air in between snorts, we couldn't stop laughing. When my cousin and I weren't watching the comedies, he would make up his own zany antics. In truth, all he had to do was tell that piano story. *After all, he sort of looked like Laurel.*

I really looked forward to family reunions at my cousin's house. They offered me a chance to do what I loved most, laugh.

Laughter is what first attracted me to my husband when we met. I was twenty-two, and he was twenty-five. Tom possessed a remarkable talent that no one could rival: an impeccable Popeye impersonation. "Well blow me down, Olive," he'd spout off when I least expected it, followed by that infectious "A-gah-gah-gah-gah-gah-gah!" laugh. I always dissolved into starry-eyed laughter, charmed by his humor. *He also sort of looked like Popeye.*

I was happy to marry someone who could make me laugh, because somewhere along the way in life, I had stopped laughing. At first, I didn't notice the shift. It must have happened gradually, slipping away before I entered my teenage years.

When I was around ten years old, frequent bouts of unexplained illness began to plague my mother. In my journals, I called it "Mommy's sickness." At times, the symptoms became so severe, my mother turned into a stranger who hallucinated about her surviving children being dead. I had no way or time to process what I observed. I was busy changing her bed sheets and trying to learn how to cook.

One day, our pastor came to our home to visit. As my mother lay in our darkened living room, he tried to console her. She was not very coherent, so he didn't stay long. When he walked out of the living room and into our kitchen, I overheard him tell my father, "Orville, she's not going to make it." I was terrified.

In a moment of desperation, when even the doctors had given up, my father called a friend. We knew she had been praying fervently for us, but unfortunately, she wasn't available to come at that dire moment. We sat in silence and cried. We sure could have used the presence of a friend.

Then, within just a few short moments, the phone rang. My father, trying to regain his composure, picked up the receiver.

"Change of plans, I'm coming over," said our friend who he had just called.

"Thank you," was all my father could get out. Crumbling under the weight of emotion, he hung up the phone. Taking a seat at the table, he folded his arms and buried his face in his hands. I had never seen him cry like that.

Financial struggles also loomed over our family in those years. The mounting bills began to accumulate and the farm work suffered as my father tried to juggle everything. A financial advisor came to visit us at our farm one day and I overheard him telling my mother at her bedside that everything would be okay. But things weren't okay.

The illness, stubborn and relentless, often necessitated prolonged hospital stays, prompting countless arduous journeys to Philadelphia. In that bustling city, renowned doctors conducted a battery of extensive tests on my mother, leaving no stone unturned in their pursuit of answers.

In these tumultuous years, I spent many hours practicing the piano. I was grateful for the comfort the music brought. It provided a healthy distraction and gave me something to work toward as I perfected my technique and developed my ear. But beyond that, the trials of illness, lack of money, and the nagging sadness that permeated the air prevented me from experiencing real joy. As an adult, this manifested mostly in my songwriting. Though it was unintentional, it was undeniable—and sometimes even embarrassing.

As we curated songs for my Christmas album, the glaring void of joy in my life was something I could no longer ignore. I realized that for uplifting songs to counterbalance the melancholic ones, I needed another song, preferably something happy.

Seated at my mother's Wurlitzer piano, I started the search for a joyful song. Perhaps it would be an instrumental piece, leaving the joyous lyrics to another wordsmith. All I needed was a melody that exuded happiness.

"Joy to the World" stood out as an obvious choice. Intrigued by the nuances of the song and its history, I started studying the life of the composer, Isaac Watts. I was fascinated to learn that Watts began writing songs out of discontent with the lyrics of his time. When his father grew weary of his complaints, he challenged his son to do something about it. Isaac took up the challenge and started crafting a new hymn every week for two years.

Among the countless lyrics Watts penned throughout his lifetime, "Joy to the World," crafted in 1719, became a cornerstone carol, drawing inspiration from the poetic verses of Psalm 98. A hundred years later, Lowell Mason, a music teacher from Boston, discovered the lyrics and composed a musical arrangement for it. Due to its release during the Christmas season in 1848, it rapidly gained popularity and eventually became the most widely published Christmas carol in America.

An intriguing aspect of "Joy to the World"—a unique observation that only a songwriter would notice—was that the initial descending scale of its melody set a playful tone right from the start. Playful felt like a close cousin of joy. I'd take it! Then, in just six syllables, the tune bounced back to its original note and started to descend again.

One of my favorite lines from Watt's song is "wonders of His love." Reflecting on this tender lyric phrase, embedded in a song about joy, I sensed that it held a significant mystery. What if love and joy are inseparable? Perhaps if I could just wrap my heart around the wonder of love, joy would naturally follow.

This brought to mind the words of the epigraph that opened this story, "I have not seen anyone dying of laughter, but I know millions who are dying because they are not laughing." Though laughter isn't necessarily joy, it has a strong connection to it. In fact, as Dr. Kataria indicated, the lack of laughter can be life-threatening.

It dawned on me that the absence of joy (and laughter) in our lives had dire consequences. It was like the unidentified illness my mother suffered from. Until we knew what was wrong, we could only address the symptoms.

Since that pivotal year of 1999, when I made the radical decision to give Christmas a miss, I was beginning to address the root of my sadness. Through reflection, I had inadvertently discovered an eye-opening truth; love and joy are virtually inseparable. Perhaps this was part of the "wonders" of God's love.

The wonders didn't stop at love. They invited me to rediscover joy ... laughter ... the emotions I exhibited in the first six months and the early years of my life, before life unleashed itself. With a sense of hope, I settled on "Joy to the World" as my joyful contribution to my Christmas album.

How should I start my arrangement? I wondered. Finding a creative way to start a song can be challenging.

Experimenting with various intro ideas, I looked for some kind of surprise beginning. The initial lines of the chorus melody from one of my non-Christmas songs checked all the boxes, "be joyful." This seemed ironically appropriate! Why not borrow from myself?

Further investigation into the origins of "Joy to the World" revealed a delightful surprise: the merry lyrics weren't originally crafted as a Christmas song. Imagine that! Isaac would be pleased to know that I played his tune not only in December, but all year long.

With a splash of Gershwin's brilliance woven into the fabric of the final song arrangement, I couldn't help but feel a playful twinkle reminiscent of the laughter-filled Laurel and Hardy days. I could almost envision Isaac Watts himself gleefully embracing my exuberant rendition.

Joy to the World³

by George Frideric Handel | Isaac Watts

Joy to the world the Lord is come

Let earth receive her King

Let ev'ry heart prepare Him room

And heav'n and nature sing

And heav'n and nature sing

And heav'n and heav'n and nature sing

Joy to the earth the Savior reigns

Let men their songs employ

While fields and floods

Rocks hills and plains

Repeat the sounding joy

Repeat the sounding joy

Repeat repeat the sounding joy

No more let sins and sorrows grow

Nor thorns infest the ground

He comes to make His blessings flow

Far as the curse is found

Far as the curse is found

Far as far as the curse is found

He rules the world with truth and grace

And makes the nations prove

The glories of His righteousness

And wonders of His love

And wonders of His love

And wonders wonders of His love

5.

What If?

Divine moments happen right under our nose.

—Frances Drost

The air was filled with a tangible warmth, and the festive decorations offered a gentle invitation throughout the church. The poinsettias, with their velvety leaves and fiery blooms, mirrored the passion and creativity that was emerging in me. It had been an extraordinary time for me, since that pivotal moment in the Christmas shop earlier that year. I was now approaching Christmas in a whole new way, free from the usual trappings and commercialism. This was a season of rebirth and renewal.

It was December 22, and I was sitting in the sanctuary at my church. Thanks to my earlier decision to skip Christmas, I felt a renewed sense of appreciation for the upcoming holiday season. I listened attentively as my pastor spoke, absorbing his words. Although, I confess, I would zone out for a moment here and there with my thoughts often turning to songwriting. At home, in my studio, ideas had recently been cascading over me like a gentle flurry of snowflakes, each one distinct and filled with its own story. The morning air often crackled with the electrifying energy of possibility, as if the snowflakes carried whispers of inspiration that only the keenest ears might hear. I wanted to be receptive to the whispers.

Mornings were my most productive time of the day. With pen in hand and melodies dancing in my mind, I poured my heart into writing music, hoping I could do justice to my newfound experience around Christmas.

Simultaneously, I found myself preparing to record my very first album, a labor of love that was going to be titled *Under the Big Blue Sky*. It was as if I was giving birth to twins: the birth of my music and the birth of a newly acquired sense of Christmas self, both intricately connected.

As if to snap me out of my inspired reverie, the pastor turned our attention to a seemingly insignificant character in the Christmas story: the innkeeper. Traditionally depicted as the negligent figure who turned away Mary and Joseph, the innkeeper had become a symbol of missed opportunities and the perils of a crowded existence. Bad innkeeper! Yet, Pastor Terry's words wove a different narrative. He painted the innkeeper not as a villain, but as a reflection of our own lives—constantly bustling and filled to the brim with obligations and responsibilities. The inn-keeper, it seemed, was not the embodiment of callousness, but rather a reflection that acknowledged the conundrum we all face in making space for the sacred in our busy lives.

Instead of condemning the innkeeper for his lack of foresight or compassion, he emphasized the busyness of life and the overwhelming demands on our time and attention. It struck a chord. In that moment, an astounding realization dawned on me, while I may not turn away the weary travelers like the innkeeper, my own inn is full. Whether it be life's demanding rush and the ceaseless clamor for my attention, or the sadness that lingers years after a loved one's passing, a full inn, regardless of its occupants, is still full.

As I left the church after the service was over, a sense of anticipation surged through me, eager to transcribe the emotions stirred up from my pastor's sermon onto paper. This song couldn't be a mere composition; it had to encapsulate the very essence of the revelation I had just experienced. It had to be in a minor key; it had to convey the deliberate choice that reverberated with the weight of the message.

Arriving home, I settled into my favorite place—in front of my precious piano. Fortunately, the first draft of chords, melody, and lyrics melded together in near-perfect symmetry, crafting a vivid portrayal of the innkeeper's perspective and my own delicate struggle to find room for the sacred in a crowded world.

It occurred to me, as I pondered the narrative further, that surely the innkeeper and King Herod must have experienced a tinge of remorse as the holy family quietly slipped away from their watchful gaze. What if a divine encounter had passed them by? What if they somehow sensed this in retrospect? These contemplations became the soul-stirring chorus of my song, and while I chose to shift the chords to a major key to provide a respite from the minor mood, the latter half of the chorus returned to the haunting strains of the minor, amplifying the introspective journey.

When I shared the song with my producer, Eric, he offered valuable feedback. He cautioned that in minor keys, original songs were not typically embraced by audiences seeking the familiar classics that evoke holiday cheer. They wanted songs that would transport them to a place of joy and inspiration. People want the tried-and-true classics that whisk them away to a land of sugarplum dreams and tinsel-filled wonder.

Despite Eric's cautious words, I refused to relinquish my belief in the song's potential. With a young writer's I-love-my-song determination and a slight touch of self-doubt, I clung to the hope that "What If" would find a home on my Christmas album.

I'm happy to say that, thanks to Eric's musical finesse and willing support, the song indeed found its rightful spot among the other holiday tracks. He had become my trusted producer and champion on my musical journey. He somehow skillfully balanced the delicate act of challenging my unconventional choices while nurturing my artistic instincts. His guidance and encouragement served as the foundation of our collaboration, even though he couldn't resist playfully teasing me about my affinity for minor key songs.

While the song retains its serious and weighty nature, it also sparks delightful moments of lightheartedness on the stage, which spill over into the audience. One winter evening, as I sang before an eager crowd of women at a Christmas event, I gave this song extra special treatment. I slowed the tempo. Took my time articulating the words, letting them seep into the corners of the room. Suddenly, I stopped, struck by a horrifying realization—I had completely jumbled the lyrics. Instead of narrating the tale of the innocent baby Jesus, I had unintentionally cast Mary and Joseph as the fierce assassins! Talk about a major mix-up!

I couldn't help but cringe at my blunder, feeling like King Herod himself in that moment. Yet, to my surprise, the audience didn't respond with disappointment or judgment. In fact, quite the opposite! A wave of chuckles swept through the room as they embraced the hilarious mishap. In that moment, as their eyes sparkled with understanding, I knew that my journey as an artist, a musical messenger of truth and Christmas beauty, had only just begun. I was learning that I didn't have to be perfect to connect with people.

And in that sacred space, surrounded by kindred spirits, I wondered if perhaps the true spirit of Christmas lies not in the perfect melodies or flawless performances, but in the vulnerable moments, the shared laughter, and the ability to find room for the sacred in the crowded inn of our lives.

What If?

by Frances Drost

A long time ago in a busy little town
A tired traveling couple made their way into a crowd
All that they wanted was some quiet rest and peace
Lay their head on a pillow that's all they'd really need

He must have been busy the man who kept the inn
When they asked for a place to stay
He'd nothing left to give
All of my rooms are full in a weary voice he said
Just as they walked away
You could see him hang his head

What if that's heaven knocking at my door
What if I'm missing all that He came here for
Something in the air tells me I should care
What if that's heaven at my door

Wise men are searching as they look into the sky
A star in the heavens will surely lead them right

They want to worship

When they find the newborn babe

Do you know where we'll find Him

Can you help us find the way

A king in a palace too proud to bear the news

Sent a group of soldiers said he'd like to worship too

But all that he wanted was to slay the newborn King

All alone in the darkness I wonder if he thinks

What if that's heaven knocking at my door

What if I'm missing all that He came here for

Something in the air tells me I should care

What if that's heaven at my door

How many times in the story of our lives

Heaven comes in a hidden way we never recognize

What if that's heaven knocking at my door

What if I'm missing all that He came here for

Something in the air tells me I should care

What if that's heaven at my door

6.

Portraits of White

*Snow is God's reminder of what grace was designed
to look like. It doesn't pick and choose where it falls;
it covers everything.*

—Unknown

A s I reflect on the journey of creating the song and the album, *Portraits of White*, I am reminded of a childhood winter memory stemming from life on the farm. In the quaint little town of Newville, Pennsylvania, our sprawling farm held countless treasures, but my fondest moments always revolved around the snow. It was during those magical nights, with flakes descending from the sky, that a simple pole light beside our red barn became a beacon of anticipation.

My father, a wise and loving man, revealed a charming secret to me. Inside our grand farmhouse, which was quite a distance from the barn, there was a switch that, when flipped, would light up the pole light beside the barn. This gentle glow enticed us with its focal point of the landscape, drawing us closer into it. The light not only helped us to determine if it was still snowing, but how much it had snowed. If it covered our footprints made from earlier trips to the barn for chores, we knew the snow was deepening.

In those serene winter moments, I was completely mesmerized by the sheer beauty and peaceful ambiance that enveloped me. My father shared my child-like enthusiasm for snow, and I believe his joyous spirit is one of the reasons I hold such an affection for it. The memory of those magical moments, with snow covering the ground and the soft glow of the pole light, as my father and I watched the waltz of snowflakes from the window, stays with me even now.

One day, long before the *Portraits of White* album existed, my phone rang. It was a local music producer who called to tell me that an anonymous, generous investor was offering scholarships to local artists for their recording endeavors. To my astonishment, they believed I possessed the talent for recording, or "the chops," as they say, based on a song I had recorded at their studio. The song, "Big Blue Sky" had been a gift to my sister for her 40th birthday.

As they say in Nashville, it all begins with a song.

The day I penned "Big Blue Sky" I stood at the departure gate of Harrisburg International Airport (in the pre-9/11 era), fixated on my sister's departing plane. In that poignant moment, she was soaring away from me, bound for Canada, back to where she lived.

Goodbyes have always been difficult for me, especially with my siblings. Among all the people in the world, my brother and sister hold a place in my heart that no one else can enter. The untimely deaths of two of our brothers, especially Nathan who drowned, led to a strong attachment to my remaining two older siblings for most of my childhood. When they both left home before I reached my teenage years, I suffered from frequent bouts of loneliness.

My mother, in her attempts to console me, would often express regret for Nathan's tragic drowning. She seemed to recognize the missed opportunity for him to be my constant companion, given the mere year and a half that separated us. It wasn't really a direct apology, because no one was to blame, but rather a contemplative acknowledgment that life could have been different for all of us.

Losing Nathan had a devastating and long-term impact on all of us. He had a remarkable ability to make everyone laugh, a trait that endeared him to the entire family. Our family unit never felt complete after his passing, especially as my older siblings moved away. The void became even more pronounced during the holiday season. As a result, every moment spent with my siblings during their visits became precious, and it made saying goodbye incredibly painful. Despite my ability to suppress tears in front of my older siblings, as soon as they disappeared from view, I turned into a weeping willow, overcome by emotions I could no longer hold back.

Back at the airport, standing there watching my sister fly away, in the midst of my sadness, a sympathetic nod of understanding came my way, in the form of a song. In between gasps and sobs, I instinctively felt that the song would be her birthday gift.

"Into the big blue sky

I watch you fly away

Fighting the tears

I walk

And feelings go running by

But here in my heart

I know

Though there are many miles to go

We'll be forever friends

Under the big blue sky"

How sweet it would have been to know at the time that the song "Big Blue Sky" would become the title track for my first album, *Under the Big Blue Sky*. It was that song that finally set my dream of recording into full motion.

However, just as we were gearing up to record the song, I fell ill with strep throat, forcing us to postpone the vocal recording date. Vocal recovery cannot be rushed, and the delay was torturous. Time was not on our side, as the studio had other projects lined up. Despite not feeling fully prepared, we had to press forward and record my song. This was not how dreams were supposed to go.

Armed with cough drops and tissues on a cold January day, I summoned the strength to drive to the studio. On that brisk morning, the landscape was adorned with a dazzling layer of white following a night of heavy snowfall. The blue mountains covered in white blankets surrounded me, lifting my spirits. I drove in silence slowly down the silvery ribbon of road. So much to take in. Then, as if bringing me a gift, I began to hear whispers. Lyrics fluttering in the distance. Like little messengers of inspiration, the gentle snowy winter winds whisked the lyrics across the fields, bringing them to me, wanting me to notice them.

Enthralled by the powdery white scenes of fresh-fallen snow, I hastily jotted down the words, "whispery winds of winter white," before they could vanish into the wintry atmosphere. And in the winter splendor, the song "Portraits of White" crystalized.

As time passed, this snow-inspired song grew and flourished until it finally transformed into the remarkable collection of songs that now form the *Portraits of White* album. Despite the album taking another fourteen years to materialize, as I wrote it I sensed that this snow song was special. As a dreamer of grand dreams, I could already hear the recorded version in my head, a rendition reminiscent of Enya, the Irish singer-songwriter. Like a young woman who carefully tucks her treasures in a hope chest, I stowed this one away in my prized notebook of songs.

While I was working on my *Under the Big Blue Sky* album, a wonderful opportunity presented itself at the studio where we were recording. As I spent months in the studio with the producer, fully immersed in the recording process, I had the privilege of observing and learning the art of recording. Back at home, I dedicated countless hours in my personal studio, experimenting with multiple vocal tracks, layering them to capture that distinctive, ethereal Enya sound I had discovered and come to admire. While blending the artistic styles of a musician living across the ocean posed its challenges, I was determined to infuse her influence into my own musical expression. It was during this time that I created an early demo of the song "Portraits of White."

Years later, when I met the President of Creative Soul Records, Eric Copeland, in Nashville, I expressed my deep admiration for Enya's music. Unfortunately, he didn't perceive any of the songs I presented to have the essence of Enya's style. To his credit, he was right. However, he didn't know I had the hidden gem of "Portraits of White," tucked away, waiting for its moment to shine. Until then, we had been focused on a new album, *Inside Things*. But I held on to my dream of doing a Christmas project.

By 2009, *Inside Things,* my fourth album (and first album under Eric's supervision), began receiving air time on radio stations throughout the United States. Eric suggested we focus on marketing that album instead of pursuing my much-desired Christmas project. Trusting his wisdom, I put Christmas on the back burner. In an email exchange with Eric, I shared my love for Enya's music and my vision of creating a Christmas CD:

"One of the songs I like and would want to put on it is called 'Portraits of White.' It's about snow ... I think it'd make a great idea for CD cover designs with snow scenes?? It would have an Enya flair to the song the way I hear it in my head. I'd want to include some other fun old snow songs on it and maybe gear it around winter more than Christmas????"

He replied:

"Yes, this should go on it. We'd need better orchestral sounds, but the vocals are cool. You definitely have a voice that sounds good doing it. Not everyone's does."

I felt like doing an Irish jig.

As a songwriter, I've learned that it's a natural progression to write songs as you process life, death, birth, hellos, and goodbyes. Though I had been writing a lot of songs around my journey with the holidays and grief, I also had a quirky side and a child-like love for snow that showed up in my songwriting. So when it came time to choose the title track for my Christmas album the song "Portraits of White," seemed like the best title for reflecting the winter seasons of my life, both the sad and the fun.

I also finally got to do my Enya thing.

Portraits of White

by Frances Drost

Frolicking frills of falling flakes

Dressing the earth in silk and lace

Dazzling delicate garments of snow

Are warming the earth in the midst of the cold

These are the portraits of white

Whispery winds of winter white

Dancing across the star-lit night

Twirling and swirling and sweeping the lane

Whisking the blues of the season away

These are the portraits of white

Shimmering rays of shining sun

Making the winter seem like fun

Carving and melting a bend in the snow

Wanting a friend who will see where it goes

These are the portraits of white

7.

Christmas in Black and White

The piano keys are black and white, but they sound like a million colors in your mind.

—Maria Cristina Mena

Year after year, I found myself both relieved and still somewhat exhausted as the holiday season came to an end, until 1999 when I skipped Christmas and discovered how I could paradoxically draw closer to it.

This discovery somehow left me craving a repeat experience each December, similar to the exhilaration of a gold miner returning to the mountains, driven by a desperate desire to pan for more precious treasures. Although I've never experienced the life of a gold miner firsthand, the insatiable longing they embody resonates with the earnest desire awakened within me. Who wouldn't want more gold?

However, even after all the soul work I dedicated myself to that year in my quest for joy, I discovered that it was still remarkably effortless to get caught up in the frenzy of the holiday season year after year. It dawned on me that an annual revitalization was essential. The pursuit of authentic Christmas joy would be an annual pilgrimage, one that I would pursue relentlessly. For as long as the holiday season exists (I mean, it's probably not going away, right?), I'll always feel the need to rejuvenate and renew my spirit, keeping true joy alive and vibrant.

I pondered the idea of an instrumental arrangement on the piano that would mirror the marathon-like nature of the holidays. It would be a medley of songs that would capture the resolve to evade stress, the tension of not being able to do so, and the constant struggle to stay ahead of it all. It would encompass the tug of war within us, striving to make each passing year surpass the previous one—the push and pull that defined Christmas. The emotions of Christmas would be channeled through the eighty-eight black and white keys of the piano, minor and major chords, and fast and slow melodies, creating a dense and intricate tapestry of sound.

Sitting down at my mother's Wurlitzer piano, I contemplated a medley. The opening strains of "Silent Night" beckoned and seemed to serve as a fitting beginning. I started to play, the octaves resounded in both hands, symbolizing unyielding determination. The bass notes, with their commanding presence, seemed to whisper, "Stop. Pay attention to this." How I adored those bass notes.

Midway through the beginning of the medley, I playfully crossed my hands, adding a visual element to keep things interesting, just for the sheer joy of it. At concerts, sometimes I would hear the audience express their interest in sitting where they could watch my fingers. I kept this in mind, letting it guide my approach.

With my right hand positioned to take the melodic lead, I maintained an eighth-note pattern with my left, resisting the temptation to hasten the pace. The melody I played with my right hand acted as an anchor, holding the rushing tide at bay. Hold steady, I reminded myself.

Following the serene tranquility of "Silent Night," I transitioned into a new pattern by modulating upward—which basically means I went up a key. The act of changing keys and tempos carries an unmatched thrill, evoking a feeling of excitement and momentum.

The exhilaration of the Christmas season began to flow through me as I launched into a light-handed rendition of "Angels from the Realms of Glory." The higher registers of the piano seemed to dance beneath my fingertips, evoking the sensation of joyful angels, caught up in the excitement of announcing the arrival of a newborn King.

A sense of restraint gently pulled me back as I shifted to the lower registers and incorporated right-hand octaves for the "come and worship" chorus. It felt more like a peaceful winter scene, where a carriage glides through the snowy landscape, its horses guided with grace and poise.

This reminder encouraged me not to yield to the impending frenzy of holiday busyness too soon.

Propelled by a different melody and a swifter tempo, a surge of energy took hold. The horses, once steady, suddenly galloped freely, mirroring the spirited performance of "Angels We Have Heard on High." How could one resist the urge to rush about after witnessing a host of heavenly beings in chorus, their radiant presence illuminating the sky?

As I transitioned the medley into "God Rest Ye," I gave in to the up-tempo nature combined with the minor key and the ever-true lyrics "oh tidings of comfort and joy." It felt like I was tightly holding on to the reins, trying to steer the wild horses of holiday emotions—excitement, hope for a better future, anticipation, eagerness, mixed together with concerns, fears, and the overwhelming weight of a demanding schedule. Despite the chaotic ride, there was a strange satisfaction in letting my fingers join the spirited dance on the piano keys.

Eventually though, everyone needs a rest.

Taking stock of my hurried state, I gradually slowed my playing down, almost coming to a halt. With renewed resolve, I steadied my team of fingers into a gentle, flowing feel, inviting serenity through the familiar strains of "What Child Is This?"

The original resoluteness of "Silent Night" resurfaced, accompanied by the lingering presence of the haunting minor key, shifting back and forth between minor and major. Tension and peace intertwined. Resolve and release wrestled within me. I pulled the music back, but it seemed to compel itself forward one last time. A gentle prompting: "Haste, haste to bring him laud—the babe, the son of Mary."

When it came time to compile all the songs for my *Portraits of White* album, we knew we needed someone extraordinary to give the songs their final, impeccable shine. That's when we enlisted the amazing talents of Brian Green. Brian's list of accomplishments, including GMA Dove Awards and a Grammy nomination, spoke volumes about his undeniable talent. He served as an arranger, producer, and musician, collaborating with esteemed names such as Cindy Morgan, Twila Paris, Holly Near, Phil Driscoll, and Carman, among others. He had also assumed the role of Stephen Curtis Chapman's tour musical director, captivating audiences nationwide with his musical prowess. In spite of his demanding schedule, he continued to work on projects for other artists, including mine.

Aside from the impressive list of artists Brian worked with, my producer loved his music. Once I heard what Brian could do with a song, I was a fan too. It was the way he played the piano, the way he added such sparkle to every song. Brian didn't just feel like a collaborator; he felt like a musical brother. Thanks to the limitless realms of the internet, we could collaborate under my producer's direction, even though I lived in Pennsylvania and he lived in Tennessee.

We tasked Brian with crafting an orchestral arrangement that would complement my instrumental medley of carols that I had affectionately named, "Christmas in Black and White." As part of the process, I recorded the piano parts in my home studio in Pennsylvania, while Brian expanded on my ideas from his studio in Nashville, Tennessee. Together with my producer, Brian possessed an extraordinary ability to infuse my songs with glistening holiday sparkle.

I finally met Brian one day in Nashville when he happened to stop by the studio where I was doing the album's photo shoot. His remarkable talent was surpassed only by his approachable and affable nature in person. This added an extra layer of charm to his impressive list of accolades.

Once the full album was completed, as we prepared to bring it to life on stage in 2014 for the first time, Brian played a crucial role in the arduous task of transcribing the MIDI notes (a special language for making music with technology) into a score for the orchestra. Until the Portraits of White Winter Concert, no written sheet music existed—every musical nuance was artfully designed solely by the discerning ears of the musicians and guided by the Nashville number charts. The Nashville Number System is code musicians use to communicate and understand songs quickly and easily. Instead of using complex symbols or notes on a staff, the Nashville Number System uses numbers to represent the chords or harmonies in a song.

Tragically, on September 1, 2021, the devastating news reached me that Brian Green had succumbed to complications related to COVID-19. His sudden departure, due to the devastating impact of the pandemic, left a void in the music world and in my own heart.

Brian, your brilliance and shimmer will always be remembered and deeply missed. So many of my projects (and those of many other musicians) are exquisite because of your gifted touch.

In honoring Brian's memory and the extraordinary contributions he made to this album, I also recognize the resilience and strength of all artists who have faced adversity during this trying time in history. Their creativity, passion, and innovative spirits have persevered despite the challenges the pandemic presented and continues to present to musicians. Thanks to the wonders of recording, listeners can still experience the power of music left behind by these great artists.

As I look back on the musical collaboration that birthed the *Portraits of White* album, each piano note, rhythmic groove, orchestral arrangement, and vocal part was crafted with intention, much like a carefully chosen brushstroke on a canvas, adding depth and richness to the sound.

In "Christmas in Black and White," the piano keys, orchestra, and classic Christmas carol melodies come together to create vivid and expressive musical landscapes. They tell stories of joy, sorrow, love, and longing, portraying the rich and nuanced emotions of the holiday season.

In memory of Brian, and in solidarity with artists around the world, I offer this melodic holiday tapestry.

"Silent Night"
—Joseph Mohr, Stopford Augustus Brooke

"Angels We Have Heard on High"
—Edward Shippen Barnes, James Chadwick

"God Rest Ye Merry Gentlemen"
—Author and composer unknown

"What Child Is This?"
—Pietro A. Yon, William Chatterton Dix

8.

MOPS

*I found that it's best to find the songs people
can relate to—whether you can or not.*
—Reba McEntire

Planning a concert is a delicate dance of curating the perfect set list, carefully selecting songs that will melt hearts and create a fun blizzard of emotions. It's like bundling up a lively bunch of musically talented kids, and squeezing them into cozy snowsuits, all while making sure nobody trips over their snow pants in the process. Unfortunately, as much as I adore my little snow creations, when it comes to Christmas concerts, I've learned that people want to hear something they know, like cozying up by the fire in a beloved holiday sweater.

I used to dig in my boots, stubbornly resisting the idea, thinking I could build a towering snow fortress of originality. But then, a well-meaning caroler—a music business professional—had to give me a gentle nudge and enlighten me; even the most treasured tales and songs can use a dash of familiarity. So I've learned to swallow my pride, brush up on my classic holiday song chops, and accept that sprinkling in some classics isn't such a bad idea after all.

I now embrace the advice with open arms, (well, sort of), expanding my musical brood to welcome back those beloved classics. I'll admit, they do bring a sense of nostalgia and warmth, making the concert feel like a family reunion. Assuming it's a good reunion, that is.

One of the most beloved Christmas songs of all time is "Silent Night." This little gem has been translated into 140 languages. According to the latest report from Newsweek (at least as of my knowledge cutoff), Bing Crosby's rendition of "Silent Night" is sitting comfortably at number two on The Top 20 Biggest Selling Christmas Songs of All Time's list. And guess what? Bing's version of "White Christmas" takes the shiny number one spot.[4]

One Christmas, I was invited to perform for a delightful group known as MOPS (Mischievous Offspring Pursuers.) Just kidding. The real name is Mothers of Preschoolers. They had invited me to entertain them at their festive Christmas brunch, and I was excited for the opportunity to showcase my original holiday tunes. However, I knew that to encourage a spirit of connection and nostalgia, a touch of familiarity was necessary. So I let "Silent Night" gracefully tiptoe onto my meticulously crafted set list.

I settled in to practice the song, aiming for a gentle rendition on my Taylor guitar.

"Silent night

Holy night

All is calm

All is bright …"

"Wait a minute," I said to myself, putting down my guitar. My mind jolted with the sudden revelation. It was so unexpected that it left me chuckling to myself. I had never pondered the implications of this particular song in the context of the marvelous beings known as mothers of preschoolers!

We've all seen the sleep-deprived, coffee-fueled super-hero moms wrangling their adorable but ever-energetic little ones. Would "Silent Night" truly resonate with them in their daily battles against runaway crayons and sticky fingers? Maybe … or maybe not. I went with maybe not.

So like a snowball rolling down a steep slope, I couldn't stop my audacious idea. Why not put my own spin on this classic? Feeling mischievous, I started crafting new lyrics on the spot:

"Well, a silent night

Is out of sight

For a mom

With babe in arms ..."

I loved where this was headed. After all the serious songs I had been pouring my heart into, this unexpected twist was a refreshing change.

There was one tiny, itsy-bitsy problem. I'd never been a mother of a preschooler. Nope, not even close. In fact, I had no experience as a mother. Nada. Zilch!

Now, don't get me wrong—I'm quite the aunt. At least I try to be. I'm a proud aunt, a great aunt, and even a great, great aunt. But when it comes to firsthand motherhood adventures, well, I am simply an enthusiastic observer. I was once a preschooler myself, but if you ask me what I remember from those early days, I'd have to shrug and confess, very little.

My mother insists I played the piano by ear in my pre-school days. I trust her on that, partly because I do have faint memories of it. She even managed to capture a snapshot of three-year-old me perched at the piano keys (apparently at my insistence), as if I knew deep down this moment would be a legendary piece of evidence. So I might not have many personal recollections, but there's photographic proof of my early musical escapades.

There I was, writing a silly song for young mothers, armed with lyrics that made me laugh. But the nagging question was, would these tales and melodies resonate with the moms? Would they laugh? Now I was scared. Considering the fact that I was writing about experiences

I had never had, I decided I needed to seek guidance from a true expert.

Enter Kendra, the young mother who had graciously invited me to perform at the MOPS Christmas brunch. I saw in her the answer to everything I needed to understand about the world of preschooler moms. She was my window into their bustling realm, and I was determined to learn from her firsthand experiences. So I asked her to write down a few thoughts about what it was like to be a mother. I figured it would be short. She was busy.

In hindsight, I regret to think that this request of mine may have piled an extra snowdrift onto Kendra's mounting busyness of motherhood. Being a mother of preschoolers must be similar to juggling snowballs while ice-skating backward. (Although I can't claim to fully understand the trials of motherhood, I do know the trials of trying to master the art of ice-skating backward, though not while juggling snowballs). I never made it that far in my skating lessons. In all fairness, I was forty-seven when I started skating lessons.

Graciously, Kendra agreed to my peculiar proposition and carved out a few precious moments from her schedule to humor me.

To my delight, Kendra went above and beyond in her attempt to enlighten me. Instead of a mere list of frosty pointers or a casual chat, she fearlessly plunged into the snowdrifts of her daily life. The sheer abundance of details she provided was awe-inspiring and eye-opening. What an avalanche of information.

Frances, here's a "short" list of a MOPS mom's to do list. Let me know if you need something else or have questions. Thanks, Kendra.

- Change diapers, change diapers, change diapers
- Kiss boo-boos
- Play peek-a-boo
- Read the same favorite story a million times
- Give baths (convince toddler to get in the bathtub and then convince toddler they must get out of tub because their skin looks like a prune)
- Get on hands and knees and run trucks down the hallway
- Create LEGO structures
- Pick up LEGO bricks scattered around the house
- Keep baby from eating LEGO bricks
- Have impromptu tea parties while the dishes remain unwashed in the sink
- Search for an hour for a lost blanket or teddy so child can go to sleep
- Wake up enough to feed baby in the middle of the night (or push hubby out of bed so he can take a turn)
- Fix broken toys
- Attempt to wet down bed-head hair
- Answer questions like: Do worms have ears? Where do babies come from? Why is the sky blue?
- Discuss peeing and pooping more than you ever thought

- Tie shoe strings
- Give hugs
- Find yourself saying you have to "go potty"
- Wipe noses
- Wipe up spills (usually made on newly washed floors)
- Sing songs
- Do laundry, laundry, laundry
- Fish toys from toilet
- Wash fingerprints from windows/walls/floor/ tables, …
- Wipe crayon from walls, floor, face, shirt, …
- Scrape Play-Doh from kitchen table, kitchen floor, and fingernails
- Push swings
- Labor for hours to produce the sweetest thing in the world
- Lament over stretch marks and post-child figure
- Watch boobs sag lower and lower after each child is done nursing
- Chase toddler down the grocery aisle
- Say no more than yes
- Realize you are your mother
- Try to cook a meal that at least two members of the family will eat
- Clean up food that toddler used as a projectile from floor or self
- Hold hands

- Display a dandelion bouquet as if it were a dozen roses
- Sleep?
- Try to get a shower once a day
- Cry when your child gets on the bus for kindergarten

As I read the neatly typed page of Kendra's preschooler revelations (I mean, who expects anything more than scribbles from a mom on the go?), a mixture of amusement and tender appreciation fell over me. From the epic battles over eating LEGO to the seemingly never-ending search for answers to life's big questions that only toddlers are brave enough to ask, Kendra's list had it all. I found myself laughing, nodding, and even questioning my own life choices as I absorbed every word.

Amongst the collection of insights, one particular phrase caught my attention: "Fish toys from toilet." Oh the wonders of motherhood! I couldn't help but cringe and chuckle at the mental image, wondering if there was a secret preschooler conspiracy to turn bathrooms into aquariums. But hey, in the name of comedy, that little gem found its slippery way into the final version of the song. The things I do for laughs!

I crafted a new frost-kissed song just to entertain the group of preschooler moms, embracing Kendra's snow-globe of invaluable insights. I couldn't help but feel a sense of camaraderie and admiration for the extraordinary snow queens who navigate this exhilarating and chaotic chapter of life.

The song was a hit. The audience's laughter was worth every moment it took to write it.

Speaking of the audience, truth be told, actual mothers of preschoolers are as rare as a yeti sighting at my concerts. They're either hibernating at home, wrapped up in child care, or performing gymnastic stunts in the venue lobby, chasing after their energized bundles of joy and trying to catch those elusive moments of silence. But fear not, dear reader, for the grandmas are always there, bundled up in their winter coats, ready to rock. They too can truly appreciate the irony of a "silent night."

After a concert, I often hear the inevitable question floating through the wintry air, "Which CD has the MOPS song? I need it for my daughter!" This humble little ditty about mothering preschoolers has become a winter favorite. Can you believe it? Out of all the songs on the album, it's the one they hold near and dear, like an electric blanket on a snowy day. I've learned that I can't control which songs will be the favorites.

Now, if you'll excuse me, I'm off to sharpen my comedy icicles and compose the next potential chart-topper. Wish me luck, my friend, and may the laughter be ever in your favor!

MOPS

by Frances Drost

Well a silent night is out of sight

For a mom with little boys

What I wouldn't give

For a chance to live

In a house without the noise

For it's hard to sleep

When your toddlers creep

From their bed to yours at three

Though I multi-task

It's a lot to ask

To sleep in heavenly peace

MOPs have to mother 'til they drop

And mothers of preschoolers

Do things they would rather not

There are butts to clean

It's an ugly scene

Not quite the night divine

And if all is calm

There is something wrong

And it's not a real good sign

We don't like to fish

But we have to if

Our children drop their toys

In the toilet bowl

We don't need a pole

Our hands we will employ

MOPs have to mother 'til they drop

And mothers of preschoolers

Get real good at yelling "STOP"

Guess I'll have to wait

For the sleep I crave

'Til the kids are grown and gone

But I stand in faith

That I'll see the day

When they get a decent job

And the tears will roll

At the great big hole

My heart cannot ignore

But it's hard to see

When they have to pee

And they've tinkled all over the floor

MOPs have to mother 'til they drop

And mothers of preschoolers

Have to work around the clock

So we tip our hat

To the stage you're at

And we wish you peace on earth

And we have to say

We are quite amazed

At the miracle of birth

And we understand

When you're old and grand

And you go to bed at five

That you're catching up

At least somewhat

On the sleep you were denied

Sleep in heavenly peace

Sleep in heavenly peace

9.

Back to the Heart of Christmas

Follow your dreams, for they know the way.

—Kobe Bryant

D reams and angelic beings played a starring role in the nativity story, delivering life-altering instructions in generous amounts. Joseph received relationship advice (Marry Mary!). They even provided baby-naming suggestions (Call him Jesus!). They didn't forget to warn about dangerous routes and lurking baby-hunters (Watch out! The King wants your little one!).

Dreams are powerful messengers if we pay attention and learn to appropriately discern their meaning. They have played a significant role in my own life. One night, I had a dream that seemed to impart a significant revelation—I was homesick. Homesick for the heart of Christmas.

In my dream, I am belting out the lyrics to "Have a Holly Jolly Christmas," but with a twist. The melody I am singing isn't as cheery as the original; it has a touch of melancholy. For some unknown reason, I keep the holly jolly lyric but feel the need to change the tune.

Startled awake, the melody and lyrics lingered in my mind, refusing to fade. Was I truly dreaming? A sense of urgency made me get out of bed, and in the dimness of the night, I fumbled for a piece of paper to seize the special gift. With hurried strokes, I scrawled down the ideas, sketching little lines that ebbed and flowed, attempting to pin down the elusive melody that would greet me at dawn.

As I set out to finish the song in the days that followed, my heart bubbled up with an I-just-wrote-a-new-song burst of excitement. Adding it to my pile of Christmas tunes, I eventually sought the counsel of Wally, my manager. Wouldn't you know, his feedback matched previous critiques, even though he phrased it in a new way. "Even your funny songs are intense," he said, referring to a non-holiday composition I had written called "Personalities." *Ugh.* I hadn't noticed this until he pointed it out. I sighed in acknowledgment. Intensity was a part of my DNA.

I sought out constructive criticism to sharpen my skills as a songwriter. And yet, alongside growth, I unwittingly nurtured my inclination for intensity. How could I lessen the potency without sacrificing my conscience and creative voice? I had been taught to meticulously weigh each word, so it seemed only logical to guide my listeners towards equal introspection and thoughtfulness.

Wally cautioned me to consider how people listen to songs. "It's usually on-the-go," he said. "They're busy, after all. For instance, picture the soccer moms shuttling their kiddos. They want a song that makes them tap their feet and makes them feel happy. When they're scattered here and there, doing serious multi-tasking, who wants a song that makes them have to stop and think—especially while they're driving."

Well, he did seem to have a point.

Though it was hard for me to see initially, I don't think he was asking me to stop being intense. He was simply pointing out a pattern that needed some adjustment. Once I got past the discomfort of the constructive feedback, I could hear that he was essentially giving me the advice every serious songwriter needed in their toolbox. If I wanted to have any commercial success (and who among us didn't?), it was advice I couldn't ignore. He encouraged me to think more deeply about the listener. It was a process that required ongoing self-reflection, experimentation, and openness to feedback.

Gradually, I began to recognize my tendency to focus excessively on the serious aspects of life, regardless of the topic at hand. It almost bordered on an obsession to ensure the world understood the hardships of existence. How peculiar it seemed now that my eyes were opened to it. My original personal mission was to write songs that changed the way people would think and live. Unknowingly, I had come to believe that infusing every song with a weighty undertone would make people better. While it was a noble aspiration, I realized that not all my songs needed to be so heavy.

This brings me to the nativity story. In my opinion, the story itself showcases a contrast of joy and sorrow. In the middle of the magnificent birth of a divine-human being, a deceitful king lurked, innocent lives were lost, and the parents of Jesus fled in fear. Reflecting on the broader narrative and with the aim of bringing comfort, I penned a bridge to remind us that perfection eludes us, even in the season of Christmas. Sadness and happiness are braided together, just like the elements of this sacred story.

The echoes of that yearning and the broad scope of the nativity story reverberated in the initial lyrics of my bridge, wrestling with the delicate balance:

"Christmas is meant to be joyful

Christmas is meant to bring peace

But just like the story

Of so long ago

Where things don't turn out just right

Children lose their lives

Royal men still lie

Families run for their life

A husband, baby, and wife

Still, this prayer I offer You tonight"

Wally's critique centered around my bridge, labeling it as overly long and digressive—a meandering path instead of a unifying bridge. (You think?!) I had to sheepishly admit this seemed to be a theme in my writing. I unintentionally muddied the waters rather than guiding listeners across. Wally was suggesting brevity, a more concise link between thoughts.

As I absorbed his constructive feedback, along with input from other music mentors, I set out to rewrite the song. Just as it took time to comprehend my own longing for perfect holidays—a longing birthed from the imperfections and losses experienced in my own family—I knew that writing a new lyric wouldn't happen overnight. And it didn't.

Gradually, over the next several years, I reshaped my approach to songwriting. The wisdom of my musical mentors seeped into my creative process and influenced my writing. I learned to anchor my focus on the heart of each song, making each creation about just one thing, resisting the temptation to address all the complexities of life within a three-minute melody.

It was a long time coming, but eventually, the impact of the song sages became evident in my compositions. I crafted a simpler bridge to the song:

"Help me to be like a child at heart

Open my life to Your love

Setting aside the distractions of life

That keep me from the greatest gift of all"

Though the bridge underwent major construction, the chorus remained untouched.

"Show me the way

Back to the heart of Christmas"

What is it about the chorus that endured? Perhaps it was the simplicity and soul-cry of the lyrics. They expressed my initial intention—the core of what I wanted to convey from the very beginning.

When I began sharing this song with audiences during the holiday season, I was excited to see how it resonated with them. They didn't have to dissect, process, or strain to understand what I was saying. Any homesick pilgrim, tired of the commercialism and expectations of Christmas could relate to the yearning of finding true Christmas. I hoped the simple lyric would allow them to feel without thinking. When I began hearing people ask if I had recorded the song, I knew I was on the right track.

Wally had been right. Thanks to his feedback I had significantly changed the lyrics. The song had shifted from trying to solve the complexities of the nativity story to a simple story. A young mother was getting up early on Christmas morning to steal a few moments alone for a short sincere prayer. In the end, it was as if the song itself was answering my own prayer, showing me the way back to the heart of Christmas. It sweetly invited me to pause, to reflect, and to release the burdensome distractions that often veiled my vision.

I couldn't help but think that perhaps the dreams we have in the night really do shed light on our days.

Back to the Heart of Christmas

by Frances Drost

It was early Christmas morning

And the tree was standing tall

The presents sat

Neatly wrapped

Waiting for the touch of eager hands

She wanted to pray

At the start of the day

Remember who it was for

In the midst of the lights

Twinklin' bright

In the silence now she prays

Show me the way back to the heart of Christmas

Help me to see all that You meant it to be

I want to see You I want to know You better

Show me the way show me the way to You

All the family soon will gather

They have come from far and near

And she longs to see

Joy and peace

Flowing in the hearts of those she loves

'Cause the best kind of gift

Isn't wrapped up in tin

It's love that money can't buy

So before they're awake

She won't hesitate

To say this prayer again

Show me the way back to the heart of Christmas

Help me to see all that You meant it to be

I want to see You I want to know You better

Show me the way show me the way to You

Help me to be like a child at heart

Open my life to Your love

Setting aside the distractions of life

That keep me from the greatest gift of all

Show me the way back to the heart of Christmas

Help me to see all that You meant it to be

I want to see You I want to know You better

Show me the way show me the way to You

10.

Ride in the Sleigh

*You never learned how to eat the cherry
and spit out the seed.*
—Lenny Gault

I f music were cherries, there were plenty of cherries I wasn't allowed to savor. Remember Lenny? Lenny was the Nashville country singer turned pastor. We had quite an interesting conversation when we started working together. When Lenny discovered that my knowledge of music didn't extend beyond my sheltered world, he playfully teased me about it. I tried explaining my perspective on bad music to him, and in response, he shared a piece of advice: "Spit out the seed, savor the rest." It was his way of reminding me to appreciate the good parts of music and not let the bad aspects ruin the experience.

However, in my childhood home and faith community, it wasn't just the seed that was deemed undesirable; it was the entire cherry. Beyond offensive lyrics in many genres, even the rhythm and percussion were seen as problematic in stricter circles of faith. Consequently, I chose to completely distance myself from anything questionable. It was a safer course of action. However, that severely limited my playlist.

My limited exposure to worldly music ended up having a significant impact on my songwriting approach, as Eric discovered when I shared a collection of songs I had been working on. After learning more about my background, he jokingly remarked, "Now I understand why you write some amazing songs and some real humdingers."

Despite Eric's teasing, collaborating with him on my album *Inside Things* had been an enriching experience. It gave me the confidence to pursue another album, even if it meant enduring more "ridicule."

Delving deeper into Christmas themes, I continued composing holiday songs. My strong desire to record a Christmas album increased. Feeling prepared to approach Eric about it, I expressed this aspiration to him one day. He excitedly encouraged me to send him the songs I had been diligently crafting.

I eagerly submitted the songs as he requested, waiting anxiously for his response. After he listened, he called me on the phone and swiftly gave me his feedback—with a chuckle: "Leave it to Frances to write suicidal Christmas songs. You have to rewrite these." Grimacing, yet laughing on the phone, I smiled at his way with words. I never wondered where he stood when it came to my songs. I either nailed them or I didn't.

He had previously noted my recurring theme of death in our collaboration on the *Inside Things* album. It had become an inside joke between us—Frances and her songs about mortality. I had built a reputation with him, and now, even with my list of original Christmas songs, I was living up to it.

While contemplating my legacy and what I'd like etched on my tombstone, one humorous idea came to mind: "Do not disturb, I'm in the midst of a never-ending song edit. Send coffee!"

As a songwriter, being asked to rewrite one song was manageable. But to overhaul an entire collection of songs I had poured my heart into for years, not just penning lyrics but diving deep into the emotions behind them, felt like sitting in a therapist's office and hearing them say, "Get a new Frances."

The task of rewriting my Christmas songs seemed like an impossible feat, tantamount to rewriting the very fabric of the Christmas story itself. Where does one even begin? So I set the songs aside. They would need time to marinate. It didn't feel like personal rejection, but it still wasn't the kind I'd frame on a wall. I had a solid relationship with Eric, and I trusted what he was saying I needed to do. I knew he was only trying to help guide my writing.

Songwriting was a subjective art, but in the pursuit of refining one's craft, it was crucial to consider the insights of esteemed individuals, particularly a producer like Eric. As time passed, the task of reworking all of my songs proved to be more challenging than I initially expected, but ultimately, it proved to be a rewarding experience. Since I couldn't alter the nativity story itself, I needed to undergo a personal transformation in my connection to it.

This became the second phase of my holiday riddle-solving journey. I had unraveled the reasons Christmas evoked sadness in me and now I had to find its inherent joy and infuse it into my songs. My feelings about Christmas were so nuanced and intricate that the journey required a fundamental shift in my perspective. This process alone extended the timeline of my aspiration to create a Christmas album by several more years.

After a few years of soul excavation and Christmas renovation, I had finally rewritten the songs. I felt ready to resubmit them to Eric for consideration. I waited for his response.

An email arrived with good news. "These are stellar! Let's do an album," Eric enthusiastically exclaimed.

Now that was a note I could frame. I was thrilled... Until Eric added a twist.

"Write a song reminiscent of the tunes from the 1930s and 1940s," he said.

"Create something fun," he added, his tone insinuating that my compositions still leaned toward melancholy, despite the revisions.

This posed a considerable challenge for me. Not only was I unfamiliar with the music of that era (or any era, for that matter), but the concept of "fun" during Christmas, as you know, felt as foreign to me as spitting out seeds.

Eric was unaware of the full magnitude of my predicament.

To imitate a particular style, I would have to listen to it extensively. Such an approach conflicted with my upbringing. Then there was the problem of the considerable gap in my musical influences—a significant void.

"You didn't just grow up sheltered, Frances; you grew up in a black hole," Eric had once remarked, albeit in his characteristically uplifting manner. If Eric could have perched himself on a cherry branch and witnessed me on my inaugural trip to Nashville, he would have seen first-hand the cringe-worthy and awkward moments that were about to happen to me in music city. He would have fully grasped the depths of the "hole" that had swallowed up my musical journey.

Here's how a farm girl from good ole Newville, Pennsylvania, experienced her first trip to downtown Nashville, Tennessee. It was the conclusion of the first day of an exciting music conference I was attending. It was way past my usual bedtime—like, farm-girl-goes-to-bed-with-the-chickens kind of bedtime. But it was my first trip to Nashville, and I wasn't going to waste it sleeping. So I locked my hotel room door behind me, jumped in my rental car, and ventured out for a nocturnal escapade into the heart of the city. I must admit, I had no precise destination in mind; I was just flowing with the rhythm of spontaneity.

I found a parking spot in a somewhat dark parking lot and meandered through the downtown streets. My sights were set on Broadway—a bustling thoroughfare known for its honky-tonks and lively country music scene. Like any other major city, heads were bobbing, feet shuffling, and an endless sea of bumper-to-bumper pedestrians navigated the concrete jungle. But the heads were wearing cowboy hats, mostly. It was a sure sign I was not in New York City.

Then, in what seemed like an obscure alley beside the iconic Ryman building, I encountered a man who seemed to possess an unmistakable air of "free-spirited wanderer" or "homeless adventurer," take your pick. Without a trace of trepidation, I greeted him with a chipper hello. After all, I was a farm girl with an unwavering and naïve fearlessness when it came to strangers.

"Look over there, it's ... something ... Gentry," he exclaimed, his finger pointing towards a figure striding a few paces ahead of us. Clearly, it was someone of significance, judging by the excitement in his voice. The bustling street chatter and live music made his words hard to distinguish. But his enthusiasm was contagious. He obviously wanted me to share in his elation and recognize this mysterious personality.

I strained my eyes to catch a glimpse. The alley leading from 116 Rep. John Lewis Way North to Broadway was quite dark for any out-of-towner, in my opinion. Perhaps it was intentional since it did create an ambiance that added to the mystique of the town. The dimly lit alley seemed to make the adjoining main street pop with excitement. I, in contrast, was starting to get caught up in the vibrant gathering of hundreds of people, all animated and swallowed up in the lively atmosphere. But I didn't understand why this stranger near me was so excited.

Noticing my bewilderment, he must have sensed my need for clarification. He pointed again, describing the person in question, emphasizing their baseball cap, oversized sweatshirt, and jeans. Honestly, at that point, it could have been anyone blending into the crowd.

"Ah, Gentry," I responded, feigning familiarity, offering a token of gratitude for his attempt to enlighten me. The fleeting glimpse of the figure he pointed out quickly vanished into the sea of friendly faces and spirited country folks. The self-appointed celebrity highlighter disappeared as well. Secretly, I was relieved to let go of the charade.

I continued on my way, taking in the kaleidoscope of sights, the mingling aromas, and the soul-stirring sounds that occupied the air. The scene was alive with denim-clad individuals, an abundance of hats, guitars strumming in harmony, and the dazzle of neon lights. Trying to avoid looking like the wide-eyed tourist that I was, I awkwardly strolled along. In spite of the relaxed and welcoming crowd, I realized I was simply just another face in the ever-evolving mosaic. Lonely and anonymous.

And there, once again, I caught sight of the tall figure with the signature hat. The star of the moment, appearing like a recurring character in the lively Nashville tapestry.

As I made another lap around the block, attempting to etch the city's layout into my memory, a wave of disbelief

washed over me as I spotted him once again—the mysterious tall figure with the enigmatic aura. What were the
chances of encountering this same person multiple times
in this bustling city? It felt like more than happenstance, a
moment not to be missed.

I gathered my resolve, determined not to let this
opportunity slip away again. Despite my lack of knowledge about his identity, I convinced myself that he must
be "someone" worth engaging with. Mentally rehearsing
potential questions, I braced myself for the encounter.
What if he truly was a notable personality?

And there he was, for the third time. Our eyes met,
and he graced me with a warm smile and a nod, his hat
tipping in acknowledgment. Now what? I mustered the
nerve to approach him, adjusting my pace to match his
confident stride.

"May I walk with you and ask you some questions?"
I inquired, my voice betraying a mix of excitement and
nervousness.

"Sure," he responded casually, his height accentuated
by his long strides. Suddenly, my carefully crafted questions evaporated from my mind, leaving me scrambling
for words.

As we passed a lively restaurant with music blaring,
an awkward air settled between us. Then, unexpectedly,
someone rushed over, brandishing a guitar, and requesting
his autograph. It dawned on me that he truly was someone
of significance. But the question remained: who?

Granting the fan's request, he signed the guitar, diverting his attention momentarily. It was the perfect opportunity for me to organize my thoughts. The star-struck fan who requested the autograph suddenly turned to me as he blurted out, "Are you his keyboard player?"

"No … No …" I replied with a nervous laugh.

When the autographing was complete, he resumed walking and our journey continued. Panic set in as I desperately searched for a conversation starter. "How did you get started in music?" I ventured, assuming his involvement in the industry. A foolish question, perhaps, but the best I could make up in the moment.

"Playing honky-tonks …" he replied, as we swerved to avoid oncoming pedestrians. I was practically jogging to keep up with his brisk pace.

He posed a question back to me. "Do you listen to country music?"

Dread filled my heart as I contemplated my response. The truth, albeit embarrassing, escaped my lips, "No."

Regret instantly washed over me. Why did I have to be so brutally honest in that moment? Couldn't I have stretched the truth a bit? My admission hung in the air.

Surprisingly, he didn't seem put off by my admission. There was no hint of judgment in his expression. It humbled me to realize that despite my limited exposure to country music, he maintained a level of understanding. How could I explain the universe and total lack of musical knowledge I grew up in?

If only I had recalled Lenny's cherry and seed analogy in that moment. It could have been the perfect way for me to bridge the gap and help this man understand where I was coming from.

Oh the missed opportunities and the wisdom of cherries!

Back on Broadway, the tall man and I continued our stroll, nearing the end of the street where the river awaited. As our conversation slowed down, I conjured up some extra courage to ask one more thing, "May I have your autograph?" It seemed like a fitting way to conclude our unexpected encounter.

"Sure," he obliged, his friendly demeanor unwavering. But there was a problem—I didn't have anything for him to sign. I felt foolish for not being prepared.

"I have a poster on my bus. I'll autograph that for you," he suggested graciously. I hoped that deciphering his autograph would unravel the mystery of his true identity.

Curiosity guiding me, I followed him around the corner, away from the street lights and mobs of people to a large bus. It must be his—I hoped. He disappeared inside, and I patiently waited outside, wondering if this was a wise decision.

Minutes stretched into what felt like a song that had gone on too long. Where was he? Doubt started to creep in, stealing the thrill of the initial excitement. Perhaps this was a mistake.

Finally, he emerged from the bus, stepping down with a nonchalant demeanor. "We're out of posters," he informed me matter-of-factly. Did I detect a twinge of embarrassment on his part? It didn't matter. I had enough of my own embarrassment for both of us. Determined to make do, I rummaged through my belongings, desperate to find something for him to sign. A Kleenex, a scrap of paper—anything would do.

After a thorough search of my purse, I discovered a business card, possibly one of mine, and presented it to him, requesting his autograph on the back. (That was awkward, but I was desperate.) With polite goodbyes, we parted ways. I bid farewell to the tall man in the baseball cap, whose name still eluded me. His signature was disappointingly illegible, leaving me with no clue as to his true identity.

Having enough excitement for one night, I made my way to the parking lot, found my car and drove back to my hotel. I wouldn't have much time to sleep—but the sacrifice was worth it. I woke up the next morning and attended the last couple of days of the music conference in nearby Franklin, Tennessee. All too soon I had to head to the airport for my flight home. It was hard to leave Nashville. Everything about the music culture there had tugged at my heart. It felt like leaving home.

As I navigated through the bustling airport, making my way to the gate, I froze in my tracks. Before me, on a poster display, was none other than the tall guy in the baseball cap—the man Eddie Montgomery, half of the Montgomery Gentry duo. Named "country duo of the year," Montgomery Gentry was one of the most successful and longest running duos in country music. I had met one half of the acclaimed country music duo, just a few nights before, in downtown Nashville, on Broadway Street. I was floored. The homeless man's excitement was justified.

And so, my introduction to Nashville and its intricate music world unfolded. From my humble beginnings in Newville, Pennsylvania to the vibrant hub of Nashville, Tennessee. The differences were vast—a curious collision of cultures and experiences, yet there was a beautiful blending of worlds somehow. I began a painstaking journey to comprehend the music business, its genres, the ministry of it, the attractions, and the challenges it posed. The cherries and the seeds.

Years later, I was saddened to hear the news of Troy Gentry's, the other half of Montgomery Gentry, tragic passing in a helicopter crash. In the wake of this tragic loss, Eddie Montgomery, who seemingly dons a hat without fail, persevered in touring under the Montgomery Gentry name while simultaneously exploring a solo career. As someone who has personally endured the sorrow of losing loved ones to tragedy, I wondered how Troy's death must have impacted Eddie. These are the poignant experiences that shape the depth of a person's existence. If I ever meet him again, my questions would be of a completely different nature.

My encounter with Eddie in Nashville served as a wake-up call to my limited knowledge of country music and other genres beyond classical and sacred music. But it also gave me a precious gift—a brief encounter with a kind, humble star who embraced my bumbling and scrambling. It became a cherished, or cherry-ished, if you will, introduction to the heart and soul of Nashville.

My producer embraced my music naivety with the same gentle acceptance that Eddie had shown me on Broadway Street. In response, I quickly became a passionate student of the game, eager to learn and improve. Since I couldn't absorb all the knowledge fast enough or fully immerse myself in the music of bygone eras in time for the new song, I relied on my tried-and-true method of songwriting. I chose a topic that I intimately knew, one that filled me with excitement—snow. Since it was autumn when I began writing the song, I conjured a vivid scene of delicate snowflakes gracefully dancing outside my car window (yet another song created while driving). This set the stage for a whimsical adventure in a sleigh.

And just like my adventure into downtown Nashville, so it was with, "Ride in the Sleigh." This song marked my audacious leap into new frontiers, initiated by Eric's daring challenge to compose a song from an era completely foreign to me. I experimented with the joyous subject of riding in a sleigh. And wouldn't you know, my sleigh ventured straight into the mysterious and magical snow-covered cherry orchards!

In the end, "Ride in the Sleigh" has become more than just a song. It's become a tribute to my journey of musical exploration and a bridge that connected me to a wider world of possibilities. It's a reminder that sometimes the most remarkable adventures and encounters come from stepping into the uncharted territory of our creative endeavors.

And the cherry on top? Eric liked the song. *Whew!*

Ride in the Sleigh

by Frances Drost

Snow is falling

And life is stalling

So let's take a ride in the sleigh

Bells are ringing

Kids are begging

Let's take a ride in the sleigh

It's a great night

For a sleigh ride

Just like kids

Let's reminisce

Let's take a ride in the sleigh

Frost is biting

My toes will be whining

But let's take a ride in the sleigh

We can act like lovers

Snuggle together

Let's take a ride in the sleigh

It's a great night

For a sleigh ride

Just like kids

Let's reminisce

Let's take a ride in the sleigh

We can sing a carol

In fur apparel

Let's take a ride in the sleigh

Stop for cocoa

Pose for photos

Let's take a ride in the sleigh

It's a great night

For a sleigh ride

Just like kids

Let's reminisce

Let's take a ride in the sleigh

11.

You with Me

*We never know what horrific and powerful currents
run beneath the seemingly calm surface
of another's life.*
—**Richard Paul Evans**

I t was an unusually mild January day in Pennsylvania
and my friend was giving me a tour of her town. I sat
in the passenger seat, enjoying the ride and the opportunity to reconnect. January is the month I emerge from
my Portraits of White concert season tunnel—as one for-
saken-feeling friend described after the months of focused
planning that I spend on musical Christmas preparations.

As part of our tour, we stopped for some ice cream.
We ordered our cones to go and found a nearby park close
to the river where we could enjoy them without worry-
ing about our chilled indulgences melting too quickly. We

sat in the car and savored our creamy treats, relishing the moment and the beautiful view. I felt saddened by the lack of snow and ice on the river, but I was thankful that it was a moderately decent winter day. Of course, regardless of the temperature, any day is a perfect day for ice cream with a friend.

As we sat in the cozy warmth of the vehicle, I glanced around the parking lot and noticed a young woman parked in her van, only a car-length away. With no distinct parking lines, it felt like parking was a free-for-all. *Pardon us please.*

I kept noticing her.

She had the driver's side door open, with one foot dangling outside, and the window down. In one hand, she held a cigarette while the other hand scrolled through her smartphone. However, what truly captured my attention was the fact that she sang at the top of her lungs, above the volume of her van stereo, passionately belting out the lyrics of the song that was playing.

It struck me as unusual. Who keeps singing like that when strangers pull up so close? Curiosity got the best of me, and I periodically looked over at her. When our eyes met, I couldn't help but feel a bit awkward, as if I had been caught staring.

To break the awkwardness, I rolled down my window and spoke. "I heard you singing ... beautiful voice ..."

She smiled, acknowledging my compliment, and took another puff of her cigarette.

I left my window down. "I wonder what her story is," I mused somewhat quietly, yet aloud, my head turned back toward my friend. I was sure the stranger's music was drowning out my voice, but one couldn't be too careful.

We continued enjoying our ice cream, while the woman in the van kept singing with unwavering passion, not lowering her volume. Her demeanor and intensity raised suspicions that something wasn't quite right. It's not typical for someone to sing along with their smartphone so loudly while simultaneously smoking a cigarette, especially in the presence of strangers parked nearby. It felt distinctly unusual, as if something was seriously amiss.

Driven by my growing concern, I couldn't ignore the nagging feeling. I turned around to face the girl in the van, and to my surprise, our eyes met in a moment of shared curiosity. It seemed as though she, too, had been stealing quick glances. Summoning my courage, I found the boldness to ask, "Are you okay?"

And then it happened. She started crying.

My instincts had been right. Something was truly troubling her.

"Having a rough day. My grandma used to bring me here, and I miss her," she sobbed, wiping away her tears.

"I'm sorry," I replied softly.

She nodded.

We all fell into a momentary silence as I debated what to do next. Eventually, I rolled up my car window, not wanting to appear too nosy. Pondering the situation, my friend and I resumed eating our ice cream, each lost in our own thoughts.

While my friend and I continued to contemplate how to reach out, the topic of writing came up. I mentioned my desire to start a writing workshop in my studio, combining coaching and instruction to help aspiring writers overcome their fears and find their voice. My friend, who always championed my innovative musical endeavors, was enthusiastic about this non-musical idea. She had kept a journal for most of her life and had some aspirations as a writer. We discussed it further, and her approval left me feeling that I might be onto something.

A few days before we met for lunch and ice cream, she had emailed me expressing how much my Christmas songs had been impacting her and changing her view of Christmas, specifically mentioning my song, "You with Me."

Her words were a welcomed gift on a dismal post busy-Christmas-season-day when I wondered if what I was doing really made that much of a difference.

Dear Frances,
You asked me why/how Portraits of White has changed the way I view Christmas. It's hard to put into words, but I'm going to try.

Most of my experiences of Christmas over the years don't consist of sadness and grieving (although I have lived through and well remember that pain). However, there's definitely been something unidentified and unprocessed, as in your case ... something/some-one missing.

I remember as a child feeling the excitement of antic-ipation of Santa Claus coming ... that is, until my brother, who's 4 years older than I am, told me there was no Santa. I think I was only around 6 years old. I was crushed. From then on, every Christmas was dif-ferent. I tried to find the excitement, the anticipation, the magic that was now missing from my Christmas experience.

Over time, I began to understand and tried to pro-cess the real meaning of Christmas, but I always felt like something was missing. The Scriptures and carols were familiar... no room at the inn, the baby was wrapped in swaddling clothes and placed in the man-ger, oh come oh Emanuel and ransom captive Israel, today in the city of David a Savior has been born, and on it goes.

I respect your time of reading and studying the Christ-mas story. I find it difficult to really concentrate when I read it ... it reminds me of repeating the creeds and the liturgy by rote which I've done as long as I can remember.

The same is true with the old familiar Christmas car-ols. I like them, like singing them, but what are they talking about? What does it all really mean? What's the heart of Christmas?

Enter Frances Drost and Portraits of White. "What could a baby born in a manger know of me? Two thousand years ago is a long time away. I need more than a story." "God with us is you with me. His hands and feet are in my reach. I know He cares when you are there. God with us is you with me." I've experienced this! But it didn't click until I heard your song ...

I stopped reading for a moment to take her words in. I was in awe. The dream I had of using my songs to help others find Christmas was coming to pass.

Feeling a huge sense of gratefulness, I finished reading her note.

So this is a lot of words just to say that Portraits of White has changed the way I view Christmas, because you give voice to questions I didn't know I had. And you give answers to those questions. You tell the familiar stories in a new, intriguing, and delightful fun way ... not just through the songs I mentioned, but through all of them. I love everything about Portraits of White!

Thank you so much for writing these songs and sharing them with the world! And thank you for doing a show that is very far removed from the standard Christmas concert, and for allowing yourself to be vulnerable in front of the audience. I can't say it enough. You have touched my life in profound ways through your music, your ministry and sharing your heart and your life stories. Thank you for being you!

Many fans may not realize how deeply a note like this spurs an artist on.

Pulling my mind back into our conversation and where we were in the car, I asked my friend, "If you could write a book, what would it be?"

"I'd want to tell people it's okay to not be okay," she said.

Our conversation gradually shifted from writing to the subject of grief and blame. My friend asked about my family's experience with grief after the tragic death of my brother Nathan. She knew some of my stories and had read my first book, and she wanted to know how our family had coped without succumbing to blame.

Reflecting on the past, I shared, "My parents didn't seem to blame each other for Nathan's death."

Although our family had faced sorrow and tragedy, there was never any sense of blame among us. I appreciated that about my parents.

A memory resurfaced, and I recalled a seldom-told story from my mother. I shared, "My mother had wanted my father to fence off our farm pond. Nathan had discovered the pond not long before the day he drowned."

We were both silent for a few moments. We welcomed the silence, allowing our conversation to unfold at a comfortable pace. My friend had a natural ease about her that made talking effortless.

Transitioning from blame to grief, I spoke again. "My father once gave me a glimpse into his response to the drowning. I still remember his words vividly. He said, 'It's difficult because the world keeps moving, and we have to keep going despite the grief we feel.'"

We sat quietly, absorbing it all. There was nothing more to say. I cherished her comfort with silence—a rare gift.

Having finished our ice cream, we decided it was time to leave our scenic spot. I had a long journey ahead to make it home in time for dinner.

We pulled out of our parking space and I glanced over to see the woman in the van burying her face in her cupped hands, her cigarette now gone. Her shoulders shook as she sobbed, her face hidden. My heart ached for her.

As we headed toward the park exit, I mentioned the woman was crying, prompting us to slow down.

Suddenly, my friend felt compelled to pray for the weeping stranger. "I feel like I should pray for her," she said aloud.

Checking in with my own heart, I tried to discern my role in all of this. I felt I had done what I needed to do by speaking with her through our car windows. But I didn't want to influence my friend's decision. I had no doubt she heard God's voice. So I felt conflicted. Was it right to go back and pray face-to-face with the singer girl?

"I did what I was supposed to do," I finally voiced.

She continued driving.

"But I don't want her to kill herself," I added, sensing that the weary stranger was going through a seriously tough time. I couldn't resist speaking my thoughts out loud. In these uncertain days (are we really past the COVID-19 pandemic?), it seems like many of us are extra anxious and feel intensely hopeless.

She hit the brakes, now sitting motionless in the middle of the parking lot exit, both of us contemplating what to do.

Eventually, we backed up and returned to the parking spot where we had been before, close to the girl. My friend seemed resolved to follow her intuition, and I respected that.

"You can stay in the car if you want," she offered.

"I think I will," I replied.

I watched as my friend approached the van. Although I couldn't hear most of their conversation, I could tell that the dam was about to break.

"I feel like God has forgotten me," the van girl exclaimed loudly enough for me to hear.

She was clearly open to a conversation. My shoulders relaxed as my tension eased.

Giving them some time, I waited until the woman got out of her van and embraced my friend in a heartfelt hug, tears streaming down her face. That felt like my cue to step out and join the conversation. Opening my car door, I stepped out and walked over to them.

"My husband hit me in the jaw last night... I can't tell anyone about it. They're tired of my sh**. My grandma used to bring me to this park, and we'd walk or swing ... (more tears). I miss her so much. I have five kids ... My husband has done this before."

We asked for her name and more details, getting to know her story. She appeared genuinely relieved that we had returned. She needed someone who cared.

I handed her my card, encouraging her to reach out if she needed someone to talk to later on.

My friend and I returned to the car and drove away once again. I rode in silence, taking it all in. I had just witnessed something too beautiful to express with words.

Throughout our conversation with this precious stranger, music had played softly in the background from her van. Despite feeling worthless, stupid, sad, and overwhelmed, she had still sung.

As a musician, a sudden burst of hope washed over me. It reminded me of what music offers people.

Songs create powerful connections, reaching deep into the broken hearts of the listeners. Through the mystery of music, strangers can become friends, even without ever meeting face to face. It's the beauty of music. Somewhere out there, someone may be sitting in their van, feeling lost and vulnerable, longing for hope, help, or someone who understands.

Music gives people a voice.

Feeling inspired, I resolved to keep writing songs. It's hard to admit how many times I've contemplated giving up. We all have our van moments.

My friend told me later that after we said our good-byes, she felt compelled to go back and give the woman my CD, "Portraits of White ... You with Me."

She texted me, sharing, "The singer woman was still at the park. She smiled and seemed glad to see me. She appreciated the CD."

What a day, I thought to myself during my two-hour drive home.

The story I shared with my friend paralleled the setting in which I had written "You with Me." It was part of a Christmas program I put together while working at a church. We needed a song that connected one element to another. We were staging a drama about a homeless man, and the scene required the right mood and sequence—something gentle that acknowledged the brokenness of humanity, the loneliness of Christmas Day, and the need for more than just a story about a baby from over 2000 years ago.

Drawing on inspiration from the name of God, Emmanuel, which means "God with us," the title gave me the idea for the song, serving as a springboard for my lyrics. For years, I saw it as a song about the man in our drama, but I've come to realize that I was probably writing about myself. I needed more than just a story from the distant past. I knew the story too well and perhaps had heard it too often. Maybe that's what makes the Christmas season so challenging—we think we know it.

And in that divine song creation moment, I realized it doesn't have to stop at "God with us." It can be "you with me." It's not one or the other. It can be both.

You with Me
by Frances Drost

Sitting alone tonight at a table made for two

Plenty to share only shadows to talk to

What does a lonely soul have to do to be unlonely

At the busiest time of the year

God with us is you with me

His hands and feet are in my reach

I know He cares when you are there

God with us is you with me

What could a baby born in a manger know of me

Two thousand years ago is a long time away

I need more than a story

Wonderful counselor mighty God can You hear me

Is there anyone here loving me

God with us is you with me

His hands and feet are in my reach

I know He cares when you are there

God with us is you with me

Jesus came down to earth to live with us

And touch us

His love carries on when we give our love

To each other

God with us is you with me

His hands and feet are in my reach

I know He cares when you are there

God with us is you with me

12.

Take Another Look

Armor doesn't do much good when
you're bleeding internally.
—Anonymous

It seemed rather ironic. If life had gone according to my plan in September of 1999, I would never have visited the quaint Christmas shop where my journey took that first long pause. I also would have never written the song, "Take Another Look."

Life often had a knack for attempting to steer me away from my initial aspirations. But that's often where the hidden treasures are; like the spiritual encounter I experienced with the humble wooden nativity figurines in the Ephrata Christmas shop.

I found myself inside those store walls because of an unexpected detour. Our highly anticipated tenth wedding anniversary getaway at The Inns at Donecker's—an enchanting collection of three country inns with meticulously restored architecture in Ephrata, Pennsylvania—was abruptly shattered by a merciless stomach bug.

First striking me, the stomach bug crippled our plans the day before our departure. Tom and I had devoted months to saving for this special occasion—a precious two-night stay at the remarkable establishment. The Inns offered a range of accommodations, from cozy chambers to luxurious suites with fireplaces and Jacuzzis. We had pinched pennies and booked the suite with the Jacuzzi. We decided to take a risk and go anyway, hoping I would recover in time for our anniversary celebration dinner. Thankfully, I did.

For our anniversary we ate at The Restaurant at Donecker's, which is known for its innovative Nouveau French-American cuisine. As farm kids, my husband and I hesitated when faced with an unfamiliar and unpronounceable menu. Being a meat and potatoes guy, my husband visibly relaxed when our distinguished server mentioned Angus beef as one of the choices. He happily ordered it, and we enjoyed our exquisite French meal, savoring the experience of the upscale surroundings.

However, as the next morning dawned, our romantic dream trip began to crumble. Engaged in a leisurely game of miniature golf, with the lush green landscape of Lancaster County as our backdrop, Tom's face abruptly took on a ghastly paleness.

"I don't feel good," he groaned.

"Should we go home?" I asked, wondering how he would be able to endure a long car ride in his sudden state of nausea. It had taken me at least twenty-four hours to feel better. I knew what was ahead.

"No ... I'm too sick to travel that far," he replied, his condition deteriorating rapidly.

We returned to our room, where Tom spent the night huddled over the expensive toilet. Knowing that he preferred solitude when he was sick, I ventured across the street to explore the shop at Donecker's. Having experienced the luxurious suite and savored their restaurant, I was now curious to see what they had in store for Christmas, even though it was September.

As someone who had always been drawn to all things sparkly, it was a natural inclination for me to gravitate toward the Christmas room. However, standing there, in the middle of the glitter and shimmer, I experienced an unexpected disconnection. The contrast startled me, prompting a moment of introspection. Rather than disregarding the feelings, I chose to give them my attention.

In that reflective pause, I considered my true desires. My gaze was inexplicably drawn to a rustic oasis within the room—a small wooden manger scene perched on a shelf, standing in stark contrast to the surrounding glitz. It was in that dichotomy, encircled by Christmas chaos, that I found my answer. What I truly sought was not more sparkle, but rather clarity and simplicity.

I stood motionless, absorbing the moment.

Song lyrics began to form:

"Simple God in a simple place,

Coming near in a simple way"

It was a sacred moment and I could sense its significance.

The lyrics continued to flow. "Nestled close to a glittering world ..."

A few weeks later, one night in October, the melody of the song emerged. I was sitting in my studio, surrounded by a newly upgraded computer and daunting recording software—an unlikely setting for creative writing. My plan for the evening was to figure out how to use all the new equipment.

On this particular evening, as I prepared to tackle the new recording equipment, a melody came unexpectedly. I learned long ago that when inspiration beckons, it's best to answer its call. Setting aside my original plans, I welcomed the surprise. I shut off the logical side of my brain and opened up my heart. The tune flowed so naturally, blending with my Christmas shop lyrics as if they were meant to be together.

A feeling of elation washed over me. I sensed that this song held something extraordinary. Memories of the humble wooden figurines on the store shelf flooded my mind, serving as a poignant reminder of the many facets of God's nature. In that intimate moment within the Christmas shop, it had become clear to me that the Christ-child revealed Himself as a beacon of simplicity. Among countless ways to enter the world, He chose the path of unassuming grace.

I sat with the melody, amazed how its freshness and resonance perfectly echoed the tenderness I sought to convey. At the top of my lyric sheet, the working title stood boldly: "Simple God." In that singular instance, everything fell into place, as if the Divine had orchestrated this convergence of inspiration and purpose. A deep sense of completion enveloped me, affirming that this song had become a vessel for the ineffable truths I longed to know.

Everything about the song felt complete.

Fourteen years after I started dreaming of an album and under Eric's masterful production, *Portraits of White* finally materialized. The album's song lyrics were rewritten and approved, the sound tracks roughly mixed, and a date had been chosen for the voice recordings. I was granted the extraordinary opportunity to record my vocals in the heart of music city itself, Nashville. It was a remarkable full circle moment from that unforgettable night when I first set foot in the songwriting capital of the world, walking alongside a country music celebrity, feeling the pulse of the music industry.

In the heart of Nashville, guided by Grammy award-winning producer, Phil Naish, I embarked on a two-day odyssey in the recording studio. We meticulously crafted each song, working tirelessly to capture the raw and evocative emotions. With Phil's expertise, we honed every syllable and note, ensuring the flawless conveyance of the soul behind each composition.

However, when it came time to record the vocals for "Simple God," I was feeling unsettled about the title. It felt as though something vital was missing. I couldn't put my finger on it. Expressing my concern to Phil, I asked whether the title truly represented the scope of the song. Phil, with his wisdom and expertise, said, "It seems like 'Take Another Look' is actually the chorus and embodies the heart of the song. What about calling the song 'Take Another Look?'" And so it was.

We put the finishing touches on the album and the culmination of my vision for a Christmas project drew near. The finished album approached its release date. Emerging from my season of holiday riddle-solving, I prepared to share my songs with the world. I carried with me a clarity born from two stories—the nativity and my own.

The season of "skipping Christmas" had proven to be an immensely rewarding journey. It magnified my sadness, highlighting the irreplaceable void left in one's soul when they've lost someone or something they love. In my case, two siblings.

Holidays amplify our loss. It was the riddle I needed to solve—healing can only come when we have identified the pain.

Believing that many others secretly identify with this holiday conundrum, I became convinced that my insights and the soul-work I had undertaken could restore joy and love—the kind we all crave at Christmas. I eagerly anticipated sharing my song, knowing it was more than just a collection of words. It was an epiphany that began with the decision to pause, take another look, and reflect on my holiday struggles back in 1999.

Looking back, I can confidently say that it was indeed worth that second glance.

Take Another Look

by Frances Drost

Simple God in a simple place

Coming near in a simple way

Nestled close to a glittering world

Take another look and you can see this God

In a manger scene

See the love that was meant to be

Simple God simple love so free

Holy God with a holy face

Touching lives in a holy way

Making way for the ones in need

Take another look and you can see this God

From a holy place

Full of mercy and full of grace

Holy God holy love today

Tender God with a tender heart

Mending lives who are torn apart

Placing love where there's never been

Take another look so you can see this God

With His hand toward you

So much now He would like to do

Tender God tender love so true

Simple things

In simple ways

Are seen by simple hearts

Open yours to a simple truth

Simple God

Simple love for you

Coda:

The Enigmatic Prelude

It was 2013 when the master copy of the *Portraits of White* album arrived in my mailbox. Already, a new vision started taking shape in my mind. It whispered of a wintery spectacle, where the melodies of the album would come alive on stage, accompanied by an orchestra. A grand show, adorned with the brilliance of a live orchestra, would weave together a beautiful wintry mix of Christmas, snow, and music. It would be a blizzard of wonder, where dreams and reality danced in harmony.

Working with a big orchestra on stage would be a brand-new adventure. I didn't know what it would entail, but I could feel the excitement building as I planned and dreamed. It was a concept as delicate and intricate as a snowflake, waiting to fall from the sky.

With each passing day, the concept grew stronger, sparkling my imagination with endless possibilities. My husband shivered and quivered, feeling apprehensive, watching as the idea took shape. (To be fair, years of experience taught him that none of my ideas were ever small—or cheap!). The thought of witnessing the album's essence blooming on a grand stage filled me with awe (and a bit of terror).

The idea began to take my heart and mind captive, consuming my thoughts. "It must deliver a Christmas experience like no other," I said. A professional show with a personal touch. It would be an immersive journey, where the symphony of sights, sounds, music, and stories would bring the *Portraits of White* album to life, transcending the boundaries of mere recordings.

True to past experience, venturing into any dream, let alone the dream of building a show around my album and my Christmas journey was scary. As a child, I remember being terrified of Bumble, the abominable cartoon snow monster. But those childhood fears are hardly worth mentioning compared to the monsters of fear and self-doubt that I'd encounter as an adult trying to plan a Christmas show. The monster would manifest in the regular voice of "Who do you think you are?"

While the ink is still drying on this final page, a sense of accomplishment warms my heart. It's as if I somehow not only conquered Bumble, but I also managed to make him my friend. This fear-conquering endeavor would become the seedbed for another emotional journey—but that is material for another book.

Just as the snow melts and winter faithfully turns to spring, and fears are conquered, I trust that the spirit of

Portraits of White will linger. May it guide you through your own frosty paths toward discovery and renewal.

Until our paths cross again in the realm of swirling snowflakes and Christmas merriment, keep your mittens handy and your sense of wonder alive. The wintry adventures continue, and the laughter echoes through the snowy valleys of life.

Thank You

Dear Reader,

Thank you for joining me on this cozy and cocoa-filled Christmas journey. As we navigate through the snowflakes and sip our hot cocoa, I want you to know how much I appreciate you being part of this heartwarming adventure.

I'm eager to hear how this tale of holiday inspiration resonated with your own frosty escapades. Did it melt your heart like a snowman in July, warm you up like a crackling fireplace or help you make space for the Divine?

If you're curious to jingle all the way with the songs, you'll find them on major streaming platforms, spreading cheer wherever you wander. And for those who want to make these melodies a part of their festive playlist, digital copies are just a click away. If you're feeling extra chilly, there are also cozy CDs available–your purchase helps support my music and keeps me from turning into an icicle!

If you're dreaming of a concert where we bring this tale to life or wish to sprinkle some holiday enchantment over your organization, I'm here to make your winter wishes come true.

Don't be icy, reach out through my website, Frances-Drost.com. There, you can explore more snowy shenanigans, connect with me directly, and stay in the loop about my frosty adventures.

Thank you once again for bundling up and taking this delightful journey with me. Let's continue to spread the joy and warmth of the season together—one snowflake at a time.

Warmest winter wishes,

Frances

About the Author

FRANCES DROST is an author and an award-winning singer-songwriter, pianist and concert artist who began her own company, "Musical Creations," as a way to encourage people on their journey through life. Take years of life experiences distilled into "three-minute messages" of lyric and melody, interwoven with storytelling, and you get  the unique ministry of singer-songwriter Frances Drost.

As both a singer and songwriter, Frances has a unique way of presenting real-life experiences and meaningful messages that are gently woven throughout her music.

Having served for a total of over sixteen years on staff as the Director of Worship at various churches, Frances brings that experience into her worship leading at conferences and churches around the world. As a worship leader, she has shared many platforms with well-known author and Women of Faith speaker, Carol Kent. She has also shared the stage with Kay Arthur, Dee Brestin, Ruth Graham, Margaret Feinberg, Bonnie Keen, and Ellie Lofaro. Frances has also been featured as a guest on the Chris Fabry Live Radio Show.

Frances is a songwriter for Songs of Love—a nonprofit organization that connects songwriters with terminally ill children. She has composed and recorded hundreds of songs for the families with their child as the star of the song.

In 2022, Frances released her first book, *Inside Things, The Stories Behind the Songs*. In this book, Frances invites you into her life in a "second cup of coffee" experience as she takes you deeper into her journey as a songwriter with each song from the *Inside Things* album.

Frances has produced eleven recording projects:
- *Under The Big Blue Sky* (2000)
- *My Refuge* (2001)
- *I Still Believe* (2004)
- *Inside Things* (2008)
- *Hand Painted* (2010)
- *Windy Hill Road* (2011)
- *Portraits of White* (album 2013)
- *Brand New Me* (2016)
- *Sunrise Meditations* (2020)
- *Portraits of White* (DVD 2020)
- *Midwinter's Gift* (2022) by Double Keyed (Co-produced with Kirstin Myers, oboe/English horn)

In 2014, *Portraits of White* turned into more than just a CD project when it became a beautiful piano-orchestral winter concert featuring a mix of songs from her winter album and beloved holiday favorites. The musical extravaganza also features other talented local musicians. People call it "the highlight of their holiday."

Midwinter's Gift, Christmas album by Double Keyed, released on November 4, 2022 and enjoyed *Billboard* success, placing at No. 13 on the Classical Crossover Album charts on November 15, 2022.

On January 15, 2023, the happy Double Keyed duo learned they were nominated for Instrumental Album of the Year through Central Pennsylvania's Music Awards Show.

On March 30, 2023, Double Keyed was announced as a recipient of the Classical Crossover Album Spot Award at the Central Pennsylvania Music Awards Show held at Hershey Theater in Hershey, PA.

Frances's song "Inside Things" won Audience Pick in Round Seventeen of the Global Rising Song Competition in 2021.

Frances was the winner of the 2009 Momentum Award for "Female Artist of The Year" and was also nominated for "Inspirational Artist of The Year" at the 2009 Momentum Awards ceremony in Nashville, TN.

When Frances isn't writing and performing music, you might see her riding her motorcycle—following behind her husband—working in her garden, or playing with her cats.

To contact Frances, visit FrancesDrost.com.

Portraits of White Album Credits

Copyright 2013
CREDITS:

- Produced by ERIC COPELAND for Creative Soul Records
- Executive Producer: FRANCES DROST
- Vocal Producer: PHIL NAISH
- Recorded by STEVE DADY
- Sunset Blvd. Studios, Nashville, TN
- Vocals and editing by FRANCES DROST at Musical Creations Studio, Newville, PA (Song of Joy and Portraits of White).
- All other tunes by PHIL NAISH at StarSaylor Entertainment, Franklin, TN
- Mixed by RONNIE BROOKSHIRE at Area52 Productions, Arrington, TN
- Mastered by RANDY LEROY at Final Stage, Takoma Park, MD

MUSICIANS:

- Drums and percussion: DAN NEEDHAM, STEVE BREWSTER
- Bass: MARK HILL, GARY LUNN

- Keyboards: BRIAN GREEN, JEFF ROACH, JASON WEBB
- Piano: FRANCES DROST, BRIAN GREEN
- Orchestra: BRIAN GREEN
- Guitars: MARK BALDWIN, DAVE CLEVE-LAND
- Background Vocals: FRANCES DROST

Photography and CD Design by ERICK ANDERSON, Erick Anderson Photography

Hair, Make-up by KATIE LAEL

Wardrobe by LORI BUMGARNER for paNashstyle

Endnotes

1   The American Heritage Dictionary of the English Language, 3rd ed. (Boston: Houghton Mifflin,1992), s.v. "miracle."

2   Adventures in Odyssey, 137, "Back to Bethlehem, Part 3 of 3," Paul McCusker, Phil Lollar, December 22, 1990, 21:02. https://www.adventuresinodyssey.com/episodes/137-back-to-bethlehem-3-of-3/

3   "Joy to the World," Music by, George Frideric Handel, Public Domain; Words by Isaac Watts, Public Domain, https://songselect.ccli.com/songs/24016/joy-to-the-world-antioch

4   Samuel Spencer, "Christmas Music: The Top 20 Best-Selling Christmas Songs of All Time," Newsweek, December 10, 2019, Culture, https://www.newsweek.com/christmas-music-top-20-biggest-selling-christmas-songs-all-time-mariah-carey-justin-bieber-1476477

A free ebook edition is available with the purchase of this book.

To claim your free ebook edition:

1. Visit MorganJamesBOGO.com
2. Sign your name CLEARLY in the space
3. Complete the form and submit a photo of the entire copyright page
4. You or your friend can download the ebook to your preferred device

A **FREE** ebook edition is available for you or a friend with the purchase of this print book.

CLEARLY SIGN YOUR NAME ABOVE

Instructions to claim your free ebook edition:
1. Visit MorganJamesBOGO.com
2. Sign your name CLEARLY in the space above
3. Complete the form and submit a photo of this entire page
4. You or your friend can download the ebook to your preferred device

Print & Digital Together Forever.

Snap a photo

Free ebook

Read anywhere